LEAN

Critical Issues and Opportunities
in Lean Management

Bob Emiliani

Volume Two

The Center for Lean Business Management, LLC
Wethersfield, Connecticut

The Center for Lean Business Management, LLC
Wethersfield, CT
Tel: 860.558.7367   www.theclbm.com

Cover design and page layout by Tom Bittel, bittlwrks@aol.com
www.dadsnoisybasement.com

Library of Congress Control Number: 2007902823
Emiliani, M.L., 1958-
        **REAL LEAN: Critical Issues and Opportunities
        in Lean Management / M.L. Emiliani**

Includes bibliographical references and index
1. Business 2. Lean management 3. Leadership

I. Title
ISBN-13:   978-0-9722591-4-9

First Edition   July 2007

ORDERING INFORMATION
www.theclbm.com

Made in the U.S.A. using digital print-on-demand technology.

This book is dedicated to its readers,
who I hope are inspired to study and practice
REAL LEAN.

Preface

Volume Two of *REAL LEAN* focuses on the critical issues and opportunities in Lean management. It is intended to help Lean management practitioners gain a greater awareness of the challenges that confront us, and also identify countermeasures to common problems that leaders face when implementing Lean. As in Volume One, it emphasizes Lean as a management system and the "Respect for People" principle. Once again, each chapter is written from a practical perspective.

Several chapters continue the exploration back in time to the early 1900s which started in volume one, Chapter 9 ("The Tragedy of Waste") and Chapter 11 ("Gaining Executive Buy-In for Lean"). The Scientific Management system of 100 years ago offers us the closest parallel to today's challenge of advancing Lean management. So it is sensible to try to better understand how the pioneers of that management system handled the same or similar types of problems that Lean advocates face today. The insights from the early 1900s are plentiful and striking. What people learned long ago provides us with new insights into how we can more effectively advance Lean management.

Chapters 1 and 2 are particularly revealing with respect to the frustration among those who earnestly tried to advance a new system of management many years ago. Ultimately, the boss has to accept and implement the new system, but all too often, they exhibit a lack of curiosity or are not motivated. Both Forrest Cardullo and Harlow Person offer remarkably blunt assessments of the failings of executives given the more courteous era in which they lived. Unfortunately, most if not all of these "faults," as Cardullo called them, remain with us today. This indicates that we do not understand the root causes of the problem and have yet to find or apply effective countermeasures.

A concerted effort has recently begun to re-cast Lean as a management system in an effort to extract it from the "tool age." Chapter 3 suggests the initial misunderstanding and misrepresentation of Lean as "tools for the manager's tool kit" may prove to be very difficult or perhaps even impossible to overcome. It will take much more than symptom-level analysis of the problem and disparate and uncoordinated efforts to change executives' deeply held perceptions about Lean. Today's rapid turnover of managers, however, will further undercut this effort, as discussed in Chapter 4. Also, let us not forget that tools are what most executives truly desire because it helps advance the current state of zero-sum batch-and-queue management, which in turn sustains their inaccurate view of the marketplace as a sellers' market, as described in Chapter 5.

The first six chapters cast suspicion on the common claim made by management that "We're beyond that." Chapter 6 relentlessly drills into that claim and reveals that it is fallacious. It shows, as does Chapter 7, that most managers are not serious about learning, and they unwittingly behave in ways that undercut the Lean principles "Continuous Improvement" and "Respect for People."

We learn in Chapters 8, 9, and 10 that modern-day Lean advocates are generally following the same path taken by the advocates of Scientific Management one hundred years ago, which was not very successful. If Lean advocates want to succeed in convincing the heads of large corporations to adopt

Lean management, then they are going to have to do some things better and other things differently. To do this they must realistically assess that they are up against and create more effective strategies and tactics.

Chapters 11 and 12 seek to inform finance executives, who are typically very confident about their knowledge, that they have a lot of work to do when it comes to Lean. They have to undo much of what they know about conventional management and learn an entirely new set of beliefs about business. It will not be easy to re-think and discard long-held views, but it will be worth the effort. The best Lean transformations share a common thread; the top finance executives are humble, do not think they know it all, are willing to learn and participate in new things such as kaizen, and change financial metrics, reporting, and processes to eliminate waste, unevenness, and unreasonableness. This type of finance executive always accelerates the Lean transformation, to everyone's benefit.

Lastly, Chapter 13 describes what senior managers will have to do in order to ensure long-term continuity in the practice of Lean management in their organization. Top company leaders will find it to be quite an eye-opener.

I am hopeful that managers will find this book filled with helpful practical information, including the notes at the end of each chapter to help them better comprehend and put into practice REAL LEAN.

Bob Emiliani
June 2007
Wethersfield, Conn.

Contents

REAL LEAN

1 The Persistence of the Current State

Between eighty and ninety years ago, the leaders of the then-popular Scientific Management movement, a precursor to Lean management, began revealing their views about why most managers resisted improvement efforts. What they learned then can provide insights into how we can more effectively advance Lean management today.

The developers of Toyota's production and overall management system clearly owe some gratitude to the ideas of early management thinkers and pioneers of Scientific Management [1], an offshoot of mechanical engineering, which would later become known as industrial engineering. While it is likely that Kiichiro Toyoda and Eiji Toyoda (both degreed mechanical engineers), and Taiichi Ohno (who studied mechanical engineering) had familiarity with Frederick Taylor's 1911 work, *The Principles of Scientific Management* [2], and Frank Gilbreth's motion studies [3], these ideas were reduced to practice at Toyota through vigorous internal development by Mr. Ohno starting in the late 1930s [4] as well as from outside sources. These external sources included the U.S. government sponsored post-World War II "Training Within Industry" program in 1951 [5] followed by consultant Shigeo Shingo four years later [6].

Mr. Shingo, in his book *The Shingo Production Management System* [7], acknowledges the influence of Taylor and Gilbreth in his work. In relation to Toyota Motor Corporation, this influence is reflected in the "P-course" (production course) that Mr. Shingo taught to about 3000 Toyota engineers between 1955 and 1980 [8]. Mr. Ohno said that Henry Ford's production system was his biggest influence [9]. However, Charles Sorensen, Mr. Ford's operations vice president says he and Henry Ford knew nothing of Frederick Taylor's work and that it had no influence in the creation of Ford's production system [10]. Nevertheless, Taylor and Gilbreth's work contributed in recognizable ways to the evolution of Toyota's management system. But let's not forget that Mr. Ohno was clearly its originator, as shown by the timeline contained in his book *Toyota Production System* [9,11].

Scientific Management made great contributions to American industrial management practice in the early 1900s. As might be expected, there were some successes and many failures. The leaders of the Scientific Management movement began writing their observations of these successes and especially the failures; particularly between 1912 and 1930. From these writings, we can learn what went wrong and how observers and practitioners comprehended and characterized management's errors. Knowledge of their struggles can help us improve our response to today's challenges.

Forrest Cardullo graduated from Cornell University in 1901 as a mechanical engineer. His classmate was Willis Carrier, who invented air conditioning a year after graduating from college [12]. Not much is known about Mr. Cardullo between 1901 and 1910, other than that he wrote several papers related to machine design and heat engines and received an appointment as associate professor of machine design at Syracuse University in 1907. He wrote a book that was published in 1911 titled *Practical Thermodynamics* [13] while he was a professor of mechanical engineering at a college in

New Hampshire. The book apparently sold well. Cardullo went on to become the chair of the new mechanical engineering department at The University of Texas, Austin, in 1914 starting out with a staff of just one full-time instructor [14].

Sometime between 1901 and 1911, Cardullo gained significant knowledge and possibly practical experience in Scientific Management. In 1912 and 1913, Cardullo wrote a 3-part paper titled "Industrial Administration and Scientific Management." This paper was originally published in a journal called *Machinery*, and later reprinted in a book as part of a collection of the best papers on Scientific Management up to 1914 [15]. Cardullo wrote eloquently about management and had a keen eye for detail – particularly in relation to difficulties managers had in breaking free of the current state. He begins by providing some historical background on modern industrial management:

> "…the art of industrial administration was stationary for a long period of time. In spite of tremendous changes in our social, economic and industrial systems, we have been content to adapt or modify methods which originated thousands of years ago…. The common system of industrial administration is constructed of the surviving remains of Greek slavery, Roman militarism, Saxon serfdom, the mediaeval guilds, and various other historical oddities, slightly altered to adapt them to the twentieth century conditions, and engrafted on one another in very much the same way as the additions to [an] old [New England] house. This system of management has been a growth in which each manager appropriated those developments of the past which

appealed to him. Sometimes methods were adopted as a result of a carefully and properly conducted investigation, but nine times out of ten they were adopted because the manager 'guessed' they were the best ones. We will designate [this] system of management... as 'conventional management'... the distinguishing feature of conventional management is the acceptance of something already in existence and the choosing, by guess, between methods which have been developed by some one else." (pp. 50-51)

Thus, Cardullo laments the cherry-picking of management methods and tools in the absence of any significant thought as to which ones were better and why. He is also saying that most managers use an "arts" approach to management, rather than a scientific approach. What differentiates the two is the weakness, non-existence, or selective uptake by managers of feedback in cases where management is understood by the practitioner as being almost wholly an art (as in "the art of management"). In other words, managers who view management as an art often ignore feedback [16].

He goes on to describe Scientific Management:

"...[Scientific management] has been developed by the engineer. Scientific management aims at the careful investigation of every problem of the industrial world in order to determine its best solution [17]. It is not content to rely upon records, or upon the judgment of the most experienced workman. It brings to its aid all the resources of science... Scientific management is not an invention but a discovery. It is the application of the scientific method of research to the problems of the industrial world." (pp. 51-52)

What is the scientific method? It "...is a body of techniques for investigating phenomena and acquiring new knowledge, as well as for correcting and integrating previous knowledge. It is based on gathering observable, empirical, [and] measurable evidence, subject to the principles of reasoning" [18]. The four basic steps are: 1) observe a phenomenon; 2) formulate a hypothesis to explain the phenomenon; 3) conduct experiments to prove or disprove hypothesis; and 4) reach a conclusion that validates or modifies the hypothesis.

Kaizen, done correctly, utilizes the scientific method. We all know kaizen to be a practical process; and so too is the scientific method. Many managers ignore this and may say things like; "We're business people, not scientists! The scientific method does not apply to us." This is further evidence that they view management as mostly an art with little or no room for the practice of science – where science is often incorrectly viewed as theoretical, and thus managers fail to recognize important feedback coming from different sources.

Cardullo notes that:

> "Scientific management has been applied to many different kinds of work, and seems to be almost if not quite universal in its application." (p. 52)

He goes on to say:

> "In many shops, inefficiency has nothing to do with the

workmen, but is entirely chargeable to management."
(p. 55)

This parallels Frederick Taylor's observation in 1912 that
"...nine-tenths of our trouble has been to 'bring' those on the
management's side to do their fair share of the work and only
one-tenth of our trouble has come on the workman's side" [19].

Cardullo then describes how managers commonly misunder-
stand Scientific Management:

> "I have heard a good many men say, in regard to scien-
> tific management, that they have managed their affairs
> scientifically without knowing they were scientific.
> However, when I have come to talk over the matter at
> length with them, I find what they mean is that some of
> the inefficiencies not usually obvious had become
> apparent to them, and that they had adopted some of the
> methods of scientific management in attempting to
> eliminate the inefficiencies which had come to their
> attention. This is a very different matter from installing
> a system of scientific management, although the effi-
> ciency of a good many plants had been greatly
> increased in this manner.
>
> However, the men [managers] of whom I speak do not
> understand what scientific management is. They think
> that scientific management is a collection of best meth-
> ods... A great deal of harm is likely to come from the
> unintelligent employment of some of the methods of
> scientific management by such men, even if they are
> acting in the best of faith. The introduction of some of

the methods will often cause antagonism among the workmen, and they will sometimes prove inefficient under new conditions. In either case scientific management is blamed for the failure..." (p. 57)

Does this sound familiar? Scientific Management helped managers see waste that was once invisible to them. But they viewed Scientific Management as a set of tools and methods and not as a management system; much like today where most managers view Lean as a set of tools and techniques and not as a management system. Sure, some improvement will occur through the application of tools, but it is not at all the same as applying the system in its entirety. And when managers fumble a Lean implementation, Lean is blamed for the failure. Cardullo's passages parallel what Taiichi Ohno told us about 75 years later [20]:

"Companies make a big mistake in implementing the Toyota production system thinking that it is just a production method. The Toyota production method won't work unless it is used as an overall management system. The Toyota production system is not something that can be used only on the production floors. The belief that it is only a production method is fundamentally wrong....those who decide to implement the Toyota production system must be fully committed. If you try to adopt only the 'good parts,' you'll fail."

Today, we are finally discovering Lean as it has long been: a management system. Unfortunately, it has taken over 25 years for managers and Lean proponents to move beyond the "tool age."

Finally, Cardullo enlightens us on the causes of industrial
inefficiency that help perpetuate the current state and management's inability to correctly understand and apply
Scientific Management. He does this in a dispassionate, clin-
ical manner, with the aim of understanding the obstacles
which must be overcome. To do this, he cites three major cat-
egories of problems endemic to conventional management:
those caused by the employer (i.e. managers), the workmen,
and America's political and industrial system. We will focus
on the first category, which consists of nine items. Cardullo,
who was about 33 years old when he wrote this article, was
very blunt [21].

Item 1: Mental laziness
"The first and most prolific source of inefficiency is
mental laziness. Most of us dislike to think. While a
good many of us will devote a spare hour now and then
to the consideration of some interesting subject, no man
[manager] will, if he can avoid it, devote two hours a
day, not to mention eight hours a day, to the task of
devising and comparing methods of work. That kind of
thing is entirely too strenuous to suit the average officer of administration. In the average plant, each officer
places upon the shoulders of his underlings the burden
of detail for which he himself ought to be responsible...
the workman is no fonder of thinking than the management... He is not to be blamed for so doing, because he
has merely followed the example of the management...
Conventional management is fundamentally wrong, in
that it compels the workmen to originate the [work]
methods, and leaves to the management only the task of
criticism." (pp. 67-68)

Simply put, managers have to understand the difference between value-added work and what looks like work but is actually waste. They can only learn this by doing.

> Item 2: Prejudice against so-called non-productive labor
> "A second course of inefficiency is a dislike on the part of most managers to employ a considerable executive staff to direct the efforts of the workmen. The management balks at such a staff, and claims that 'non-productive' labor is a necessary evil if you have to employ it, and an unnecessary evil if you can do with out it. In the old days draftsmen were regarded as an unnecessary evil, and the designing was done by rule-of-thumb and the head patternmaker. Experience has shown that *Johnny Pencilpusher* is not an evil, nor is he unnecessary, and that it pays to employ him... The men who direct the work of the shop are just as necessary as the men who make the designs... The labor of the planning department is just as truly productive as the labor of the drafting department, the machine department, or the erecting department. A new attitude in regards to the employment of indirect labor is a pre-requisite to greater efficiency..." (p. 69)

In contrast to 1914, the prejudice today is clearly against productive labor. Cardullo is no doubt annoyed with the recently created standard cost (absorption) accounting systems that classify workers in ways that are convenient for accountants but foment dysfunction among company managers. Cardullo sees business as a system and not isolated parts labeled as "direct," indirect," or as drafting, planning, or production. He wants managers to understand that they need all the parts, not just some, for the business to work properly, and that it is harmful for managers to favor one class of people or activity over another. Unfortunately, we still suffer today from top managers who favor one class, function, or activity over others (i.e., those in the in-group), which marginalize the interests of people in the out-group and undercuts teamwork.

Item 3: Timidity of capital

"A third fault of management is timidity. Capital seems to be ruled by fear quite as often as by judgment. Men dislike to risk their money in something which they feel is not absolutely sure to bring adequate returns... so the present-day employer is fearful of assuming the expense incident to proper management, even though it can be shown that great gains ought to be realized from proper administration." (pp. 69-70)

Then as now, managers want bullet-proof evidence of savings and benefits before agreeing to depart from the current state of conventional management practices [22]. Another manifestation of this is the common view that the introduction of Lean management is a cost, and not a savings. Related to that is a strong desire to "bean count" Lean activities; to determine the return on investment or internal rate of return for kaizens. If the kaizen result does not financially pay back what has been put into it, then there is no kaizen. Managers who do this fail to realize their decision is self-centered and made without consideration of end-use customers. They also fail to understand that kaizen is a long-term process of learning how to improve, and that not doing kaizen means there will be no learning or improving. Inevitably the company will one day find itself in trouble, and the people will have failed to learn things that could have avoided the calamity altogether or help overcome the problems more quickly.

Item 4: Lack of foresight

"This brings us to a fourth fault of management, which is a lack of foresight. The management, in performing the work of today, fails to make allowances for the needs of next week, or the growth of next year... The lack of definite and far-reaching plans for future work is not felt at the time that such plans should be made, but it is felt later." (p. 70)

Short-term thinking is not a new phenomenon.

Item 5: Mental inertia and lack of adaptability

"A fifth fault of management is one which may best be described as 'mental inertia.' Managers tend to follow methods which have been satisfactory in the past, but which changing conditions have made unsatisfactory for present requirements. Whenever a new invention of any importance is introduced into the shop the conditions of work are greatly altered. The introduction of high speed steel [by Frederick Taylor [23]] is a case in point... in most cases the management will attempt to get along with the least possible change in equipment, and in methods of work and administration. Many men resist change simply because it is change, in spite of the fact that the change may be desirable." (pp. 70-71)

Senior managers are human and have fears and concerns just like anyone else. One would hope that managers – mostly well paid and educated, possessing a wider view (hopefully),

and concerned about the future of the business – would not
allow themselves to get stuck in the current state and fail to
see the need for change around the time that it is necessary.
Unfortunately, this happens all the time.

> Item 6: Lack of study of the industry
> "A sixth and probably one of the greatest of all causes
> of inefficiency is the fact that the management very sel-
> dom makes a careful study of the industry… When it is
> all said and done, it will be found that most managers
> want some one else to do the experimenting [studies],
> feeling that by doing so they can participate in the prof-
> its of such work without sharing its expenses." (p. 72)

A mark of professionalism is dedicated study and practice in
the field for which one has responsibility. With daily discipline and great effort, the result will be fewer errors and better outcomes. Instead, Cardullo says managers frequently
lack professionalism and act as "free riders," people who
gain something for nothing, which indicates that their prior-
ities are misplaced.

> Item 7: Systems of rewarding labor
> "A seventh source of inefficiency in many industrial
> plants is the system of wage payment adopted. It would
> be hard to devise wage systems better calculated to
> limit efficiency than the two which are in most com-
> mon use; namely, the day wage plan and the piece work
> plan with frequent cuts." (pp. 72-73)

This issue has not gone away; it has just taken on different
forms. The first big problem today is the compensation sys-

tems for rewarding top managers, not production laborers. The second big problem today is the huge gap between average worker pay and benefits in relation to what senior managers receive; and that real wages for production workers, adjusted for inflation, have been flat for more than two decades despite a 43% increase in productivity between 1990 and 2006 [24]. The most significant thing in common between then and now is that the gains have not been equitably shared with labor.

> <u>Item 8: "Holier than thou" spirit of some employees</u>
> "An eighth cause of inefficiency is one which is happily becoming less frequent. It is a disposition on the part of some employees to regard their workmen as being of a lower order of humanity than themselves... I have heard them speak of their workmen as 'beasts' and 'ignorant brutes.' No man who regards his employees in that light can be persuaded to adopt scientific management nor can he bring the efficiency of his plant to a high standard, because such feelings will unconsciously affect his attitude in dealing with his employees, arouse their antagonism, and destroy that feeling of cooperation which is the essential basis of high efficiency." (p. 74).

Today we don't refer to production workers as "beasts" and "ignorant brutes," but we do refer to each other in less colorful but still condescending ways that give people reasons to withdraw from participation: shop rats, bean counter, engineering weenie, parts chaser, HR do-nothing, ivory tower lawyer, IT geek, marketing puke, quality pains-in-the-asses, etc. The outcome is the same: antagonism that undercuts our ability to function as teams in business – a quintessentially cooperative human activity. "Behavioral waste," a term that I coined in 1998 [25], is toxic to Lean management.

Item 9: Avarice of the management
"The last source of inefficiency of which I will speak is avarice on the part of management...Not only will avarice prevent the adoption of scientific management in a great many cases, but it is also very likely to give scientific management a black eye by adopting some of its methods, without adopting its spirit. An avaricious employer finds himself coming out second best in competition with one who utilizes scientific management. He attempts to appropriate the experience of his competitor in the same spirit in which he imitates his trademarks, copies his designs, and steals his methods of work. Now while it is possible to imitate a trade-mark or steal a method, it is not possible to imitate or to steal the scientific habit of mind or the spirit of fair play, which lie at the basis of scientific management... the extraordinary performances possible under scientific management will never be achieved in the shops of the avaricious employer because knowledge alone will not lead workmen to increase their efficiency." (pp. 75-76).

Cardullo is saying that merely copying a competitor that practices Scientific Management well will not assure success. These days, we would say that copying the tools of Lean – i.e. practicing only the "Continuous Improvement" principle – is insufficient. Management must also practice the "Respect for People" principle [26,27].

At the end of this section, Cardullo says:

> "I have endeavored merely to point out the fact that such faults exist, that they can be remedied, and that before [genuine] scientific management can be applied to an industry, they must be remedied." (p. 76)

Likewise, the faults must be remedied before genuine Lean management can be applied.

Notes

[1] W. Tsutsui, *Manufacturing Ideology: Scientific Management in Twentieth-Century Japan*, Princeton University press, Princeton New Jersey, 1998

[2] F.W. Taylor, *The Principles of Scientific Management*, Harper & Brothers Publishers, New York, NY, 1911. In a nutshell, Scientific Management can be described as a system of production management that, if done correctly, resulted in a much more efficient batch-and-queue (push) production system; 2-3 times more efficient than basic batch-and-queue production. Its application was later extended to non-production activities and to non-manufacturing industries. Its main foci were "betterment" of the work and "cooperation" among the management and the workers. Some of its principles, methods, and tools are the same or similar to that found in Lean management.

[3] F Gilbreth, *Motion Study*, D. Van Nostrand Co., New York, NY, 1911

[4] Ohno's knowledge of Taylor and Gilbreth works is described by Michael Cusumano as follows: "...the 'time and motion' studies he used to examine workers and machines came from the United States. His first encounter with these techniques occurred during 1937-1938 when a supervisor at Toyoda Spinning and Weaving asked him to study the latest American management methods and to report on those he thought would be useful for manufacturing thread. Ohno read several textbooks and articles that contained a variety of ideas and theories, but nothing practical. He then decided that the best way to improve the Toyoda factory was to put the textbooks aside, go to the shop floor, and study the plant and workers in operation." M. Cusumano, *The Japanese Automobile Industry: Technology and Management at Nissan and Toyota*, The Council on East Asian Studies, Harvard University, Cambridge, MA, 1985, p. 272

[5] J. Huntzinger, "The Roots of Lean," http://www.superfactory.com/articles/Huntzinger_roots_lean.pdf, June 2005, and A. Smalley, "TWI Influence on TPS and Kaizen," http://www.superfactory.com/articles/Smalley_Kato_TWI.htm, May 2006

[6] Another source who may have informed Kiichiro Toyoda, Eiji Toyoda, and Taiichi Ohno about Scientific Management in the 1920s or 1930s was Yoichi Ueno (1883-1957). Ueno was a prominent advocate of Scientific Management in pre-World War II Japan. He was a writer, educator, and management consultant who published many books that interpreted Scientific Management's technical and human dimensions for his Japanese audience. See W. Tsutsui, "The Way of Efficiency: Ueno Yoichi and Scientific Management in Twentieth-Century Japan," *Modern Asian*

Studies, Vo. 35, No. 2, pp. 441-467, 2001

[7] S. Shingo, *The Shingo Production Management System: Improving Process Functions*, Productivity Press, Portland, OR, 1992

[8] S. Shingo, *Study of 'Toyota' Production System from Industrial Engineering Viewpoint*, Japan Management Association, Tokyo, Japan, November 1981, distributed by Productivity Press, Inc., Cambridge, MA, p. 17

[9] T. Ohno, *Toyota Production System*, Productivity Press, Portland, OR, 1988

[10] C. Sorensen, *My Forty Years with Ford*, W.W. Norton Co., Inc., New York, NY, 1956, p. 41. Sorensen says: "One of the hardest-to-down myths about the evolution of mass production at Ford is one which credits much of the accomplishment to 'scientific management.' No one at Ford – not Mr. Ford, Couzens, Flanders, Wills, Pete Martin, nor I – was acquainted with the theories of the 'father of scientific management,' Frederick W. Taylor. Years later I ran across a quotation from a two-volume book about Taylor by Frank Barkley Copley, who reports a visit Taylor made to Detroit late in 1914, nearly a year after the moving assembly line had been installed at out Highland Park plant. Taylor expressed surprise to find that Detroit industrialists 'had undertaken to install the principles of scientific management without the aid of experts.' To my mind, this unconscious admission by an expert is expert testimony on the futility of too great reliance on experts and should forever dispose of the legend that Taylor's ideas had any influence at Ford."

[11] See A. Smalley, "A Brief Investigation into the Origins of the Toyota Production System," http://www.superfactory.com/articles/smalley_origins_and_facts_regarding_TPS.pdf June 2006 and A. Smalley, "Shigeo Shingo's Influence on TPS: An Interview with Mr. Isao Kato," http://www.superfactory.com/articles/Smalley_Shingo_TPS_Kato.htm, April 2006

[12] For a brief biography of Willis Carrier, see http://en.wikipedia.org/wiki/Willis_Carrier or *Willis Carrier: Father of Air Conditioning*, M. Ingels, Carrier Corporation, 1991 (reprint of 1952 edition)

[13] F. Cardullo, *Practical Thermodynamics: A Treatise on the Theory and Design of Heat Engines, Refrigeration Machinery, and Other Power-Plant Apparatus*, McGraw-Hill Book Co., Inc., New York, NY, 1911

[14] See http://www.me.utexas.edu/visitor/building.shtml

[15] C. B. Thompson, *Scientific Management: A Collection of the More Significant Articles Describing The Taylor System of Management*, Harvard University Press, Cambridge, MA, 1914. Forrest Cardullo's paper "Industrial Administration and Scientific Management" appears on pages 49-83. The original paper appeared in *Machinery*, Vol. 18, p. 843 and 931,

1912, and in Vol. 19, p. 18, 1913.

[16] Artists generally prefer to do what they want to do and ignore feedback from critics, etc. Scientists and engineers, on the other hand, usually pay attention to feedback in the form of results from tests, experiments, etc. That is, they seek to improve their understanding by obtaining better information, and then factor that into their future work. Sometimes artists listen to feedback and sometimes scientists and engineers ignore feedback. There are components of any type of work that are artistic in nature, including management, where people may or may not respond to feedback. Senior managers who are unresponsive to negative feedback or who view no criticism as justified (the imperial style of management) stand in the way of continuous improvement and obviously have no interest in respect for people. They should not be leaders of people because they will create waste, unevenness, and unreasonableness, and destroy wealth.

[17] In the early days of Scientific Management, engineers searched for the "one best way" to do a job and typically did not seek input from the laborers who actually did the work. It was not long before some engineers and managers realized that workers possess valuable knowledge should be listened to. In time, the search for the "one best way" became more of a collaborative effort in some organizations. Also, the notion of "continuous improvement" was not understood in the early days of Scientific Management. Only later did some people realize that processes can be improved many times.

[18] See http://en.wikipedia.org/wiki/Scientific_method

[19] *Scientific Management: Comprising Shop Management, Principles of Scientific Management, Testimony Before the House Committee*, F.W. Taylor, with foreword by Harlow S. Person, Harper & Brothers Publishers, New York, NY, 1947, p. 43

[20] T. Ohno in *NPS: New Production System*, by I. Shinohara, Productivity Press, Cambridge, MA, 1988, pp. 153, 155

[21] Being blunt carries the risk that top managers will be offended and therefore not listen. On the other hand, not being blunt risks perpetuating the current state which is bad for all stakeholders. It seems that Cardullo, and many others in the decades that followed, felt that people in leadership positions should be able to withstand criticisms, and also see and respond to the merits of criticisms for the betterment of themselves, their business, and their stakeholders.

[22] This was a large part of my motivation to write *Better Thinking, Better Results*; to show, in unambiguous terms, the financial and non-financial benefits of the Lean management system. See B. Emiliani, with D. Stec, L.

Grasso, and J. Stodder, *Better Thinking, Better Results: Case Study and Analysis of an Enterprise-Wide Lean Transformation*, second edition, The CLBM, LLC, Wethersfield, Conn., 2007

[23] F.W. Taylor, "On the Art of Cutting Metals," *Trans. ASME*, Vol. 28, pp. 31-350, 1907

[24] U.S. Bureau of Labor Statistics, http://www.bls.gov

[25] M.L. Emiliani, "Lean Behaviors," *Management Decision*, Vol. 36, No. 9, pp. 615-631, 1998

[26] "The Toyota Way 2001," Toyota Motor Corporation, internal document, Toyota City, Japan, April 2001

[27] B. Emiliani, *REAL LEAN: Understanding the Lean Management System,* Volume One, The CLBM, LLC, Wethersfield, Conn., 2007

2 The Leadership Problem

*The closest parallel to today's challenge of advancing
Lean management lies in the work done by proponents of
Scientific Management seventy-five years ago. It was then
they realized for certain that their movement would not
gain broader acceptance nor be correctly applied unless
the people who ran businesses exhibited a completely
different type of leadership.*

The challenges we face today in advancing Lean management
are strikingly similar to what the proponents of Scientific
Management faced in the 1920s. Around that time they began
to realize that while the impact of Scientific Management in
industry over the prior thirty years was substantial, it had fall-
en well short of expectations in terms of the level of improvement that could have been achieved and the favorable outcomes they anticipated key stakeholders would realize.

This was due largely to the widespread misunderstanding of
Scientific Management as a set of efficiency improvement
tools, rather than as a system of management that consisted of
both principles and tools. The principle that people seemed to
forget or ignore was the "intimate cooperation of the management with the workmen" [1]. Today, in Lean management,
this idea is more fully developed and called the "Respect for
People" principle [2-5].

One prominent and tireless advocate of Scientific
Management was Harlow S. Person (1875-1955), who served
as a managing director and later as president of The Taylor

Society in New York City from the mid-1920s to the late 1940s. He lived during a unique window of time; one that allowed him to witness Scientific Management take hold in industry and eventually fade away; though parts of it still live on today, albeit in different forms.

Mr. Person spent much of his life trying to dispel the myths and correct misapplications of Scientific Management, and help people gain an accurate understanding of its principles and practices. As professor [6], and later Dean of Dartmouth's Amos Tuck School of Administration and Finance, Person promoted the teaching of "employment management" in graduate courses in 1910. He hosted the first conference in Scientific Management in the United States on October 12-14, 1911. In 1915 Person offered training programs in Scientific Management to industrial managers. The program for managers required the completion of a paper investigating a work-related problem [7].

Despite the dedicated efforts of many management practitioners, academics, and consultants over the first twenty-five years of Scientific Management's existence, Frederick Taylor (1856-1915), author of the 1911 book *The Principles of Scientific Management*, observed in 1912 that [8]:

> "...nine-tenths of our trouble has been to 'bring' those on the management's side to do their fair share of the work and only one-tenth of our trouble has come on the workman's side."

In other words, the managers were not getting it done. Up until the late 1920, the failings of managers were described as their resistance to developing a "new mental attitude of the management toward the men [laborers]," and that Scientific Management could not exist if this new mental attitude were not possessed by the top managers of a company. The "new mental attitude" was described by Taylor in 1912 as going from a zero-sum to a non-zero-sum view of business [9]:

> "...the first step towards scientific management... [a] complete change in the mental attitude of both sides [labor and management]; of the substitution of peace for war; the substitution of hearty brotherly cooperation for contention and strife; of both pulling hard in the same direction instead of pulling apart; of replacing suspicious watchfulness with mutual confidence; of becoming friends instead of enemies...is the very essence of scientific management, and scientific management exists nowhere until after this has become the central idea... the mechanism [tools] is nothing if you have not got the right sentiment..."

In 1947 Mr. Person said [10]:

> "In the course of his testimony before the House committee [to Investigate the Taylor and Others Systems of Shop Management], Taylor was asked how many concerns [companies] used his system in its entirety. His reply was: 'In its entirety – none; not one.' Then, in response to another question he went on to say that a great many used it substantially, to a greater or less degree. Were Mr. Taylor alive to respond to the same question in 1947 – thirty-five years later – his reply would have to be essentially the same."

Thus, not much progress was made in the second twenty-five plus years of Scientific Management's existence, principally because managers did not comprehend cause-and-effect relationships between the application of new methods and tools in relation to people. Nor did they comprehend the importance of the principles and how they function as practical reference points for management thinking and decision-making.

For many years the simple characterization of senior managers needing a "new mental attitude" was the common way in which the problem was expressed. Taylor and his followers did not understand this explicitly as a leadership problem because leadership, as a field of study, was in its infancy. It was not until the mid-to-late 1920s that academics began conceptualizing leadership and writing books on the topic for management practitioners [11,12].

In terms of Scientific Management, the "new mental attitude" problem transitioned into being a leadership problem in the late 1920s. Harlow Person picked up on this and wrote about it starting in 1929, in a paper titled "Leadership in Scientific Management" [13]. He said:

> "Attempts to develop scientific management have in general been successful in direct proportion to the degree to which those who have initiated and directed its development have possessed genuine qualities of leadership. And the failures attributed to scientific management have generally been failures of leadership in initiating and guiding its development, particularly the order, rate and extent of development." (p. 427)

Executives who put in the effort to study, participate, and understand the new management system will succeed while those who don't invariably fail and end up blaming the new management system, not themselves.

> "The first conspicuous weakness of leadership in this respect may be failure to realize that there is involved the problem of integrating radically different types of executives in an organization where the mental attitudes and habits have originally been dominated and set by one particular type. We know of no instance in which an enterprise has been *started* with the ideal application of the Taylor principles and an original executive staff designed for that purpose. That ideal usually comes later with a problem of reorganization to meet new and sometimes embarrassing industrial conditions." (p. 427)

This should not be news to anyone who knows the recent history of Lean management. A primary mode by which Lean transformations fail is when one or two executives understand Lean, but the others don't. In order to succeed, all executives need to develop a deep and uniform understanding of the Lean management system. Referring to it as "Lean manufacturing" will give every executive other than the one responsible for manufacturing a good reason to ignore it. Also, most managers get involved with Lean because the company has severe performance problems, not because they really want to do it.

> "... [for] promoter type [executives]... Neither temperament nor motive incline them to be interested in the details involved in operating procedures... [they are]

known as the go-getter type so characteristic of frontier industry and a sellers' market. It is this promoter and go-getter type of executive which usually dominates an enterprise in its early years and determines mental attitudes and practices. With the introduction of scientific management, however, there arises a new type of executive interested in designing a precise and waste-saving system of interlocking methods... an engineering type of executive....[the] go-getter type drives straight to results regardless of methods and cost... But while the forceful go-getter type of executive will always be essential, managers have come to realize that an organization must be balanced by the inclusion of the thinking, investigating, planning type of executive... [who] has regard for efficiency and economy of methods... Even the go-getter executive, so useful in the early days of an enterprise, must become a thinking, planning executive after the enterprise is well established as a going concern." (pp. 427-428)

What Mr. Person is saying is that different types of executives are needed for different stages of an organization's existence. Similarly, different types of executives are needed for different types management systems: conventional management versus Scientific Management – and exactly the same is true for conventional management versus Lean management. So has anything been done in the last seventy-five years to help people understand these differences as it pertains to Lean management? The answer is yes: in 2003 and 2004 I wrote or co-wrote papers that describe, in comprehensive and detailed ways, the specific differences in beliefs, behaviors, and competencies between leaders of Lean compared to conventionally managed businesses [14,15]. These papers answer long-standing questions and provide practical actions that managers can take to improve.

Person makes two other interesting points in this passage. The first relates to the "frontier industry and a sellers' market," where a company is able to sell as much as it can make. Managers who grow up in a sellers' market develop "mental attitudes and practices" for that type of market. As a business matures, competitors enter the business and change it into a buyers' market. If the sellers' market "mental attitudes and practices" do not change, then the company will likely face a "problem of reorganization to meet new and sometimes embarrassing industrial conditions."

The second point relates to managers who "do" compared to those who "think," and those rare managers who both "think and do." Person compares executives who are "doers," the go-getter types, to the engineering-type of executive who thinks, investigates, plans, etc. Possessing one skill or the other may be appropriate at any given point in time, but strengths can easily turn into weaknesses. Importantly, Mr. Person notes that the go-getter executive must develop new skills to avoid becoming handicapped. As you can imagine or may already know, the better executives would possess both skills. And by the way, that's exactly what the best Lean leaders are good at, thinking and doing.

Person continues:

> "...the fact should be recognized that the development of scientific management first of all compels the

rebuilding of the executive group so that it shall represent a proper balance of these types working together sympathetically and understandingly for a common purpose... the harmonizing of these types of executives involves the breaking down of well-established organization habits and the building up of new executive habits... It is no small matter to introduce a new type of executive and evolve (to create is impossible) in the reorganized group a new integration of habit relationships." (p. 429-430)

This is not as hard to do as was once thought to be. Please read references [14] and [15] to learn how.

Mr. Person quotes the industrialist James Mapes Dodge on his views regarding the problem of introducing Scientific Management into an organization. Mr. Dodge uttered these words at the Scientific Management conference at the Amos Tuck School in October 1911:

"He will of course find, when he [the owner] approaches his subordinates and they in varying degrees accept his views with the feeling that something can be done of advantage to the establishment, that in no case will his leading men consider that anything in this new-fangled management business should be in any way applied to them, though they can see with greater or less degree of certainty that it would be admirable for everybody else in the place. The problem of overcoming this mental condition is the most difficult of all. The very fact that the leading men of an establishment are beholden to their cleverness and independence of thought for their promotion makes it certain that they will not hesitate to combat the views of their superior, if in their judgment it seems best." (p. 430).

Mr. Dodge is describing classic passive-aggressive (obstructionist) behavior. Managers voice agreement with the boss, but then work to resist or undermine the boss. Anyone who has been involved in a Lean transformation knows exactly what Mr. Dodge is talking about. In 1998 I coined the term "behavioral waste" [16] to describe this and other behaviors which add cost but do not add value, and also described practical countermeasures [17].

Mr. Person goes on to say:

> "…[an] absence of appreciation [among leaders] that the development of scientific management is an *educational* process… [all the changes that must occur] cannot be achieved by fiat… And the educational technique cannot be that of the birch rod, but must be of persistent, patient leadership in the common discovery of laws of managerial situations which impersonally compel understanding and conviction and attract desire and voluntary disciplined cooperation throughout the organization." (pp. 431-432)

Then, like now, leaders who mandate change will certainly achieve some gains, but they will also witness significant backslide and likely the overall failure of their efforts. In addition, most change efforts are caused by financial distress or the desire by management to achieve short-term gains. These leaders fail to realize that Lean is a learning process.

Short-term thinking is not conducive to the type of learning that is needed to succeed over the long-term as Toyota and others have done. In addition, Mr. Person makes note of the strong desire and discipline that an entire management team must possess in order to learn a new system of management. The effort that most managers put into learning Lean is so small that were they to put in the same amount of effort learning to play guitar, the only song they would ever know is the one-minute beginner's classic "Ode to Joy."

Mr. Person then describes some specific characteristics of leadership that are required of executives who expect to succeed with Scientific Management:

> "Leadership is not passive; it is an active composite ability to induce (not impose) understanding, conviction, desire and action in a manner which leaves no disturbing impression of the mechanics of the induction... As a leader he must have energy, enthusiasm, imagination, intelligence, technical knowledge, knowledge of human nature, faith in people; and qualifying all of these, a special quality of sympathetic interest towards those led. Not only must he manifest these characteristics in his relations with those major associate executives with whom he has immediate contact, but also he must inspire all of them to desire and learn how to become creative leaders in relations with their immediate associates." (p. 432)

These characteristics appear again and again in cases where the Lean transformation has succeeded across the enterprise [5]. Mr. Person then observed that sub-units of corporations often do well with Scientific Management:

> "But throughout American industry are many instances of the development of scientific management, under the leadership of subdepartment executives, in the departments of an enterprise for which they have responsibility." (p. 432)

As an examination of Shingo Prize-winning companies clearly shows, there are many managers who have made noteworthy progress at the plant-level, but much less so at the enterprise-level.

Person had hope that better days would come:

> "When in the course of time these departmental managers have carried their departmental experiences to positions of top leadership, transformations of entire enterprises will become more frequent." (p. 433)

This has happened today, but not widely so, as executives from companies who have had some success with Lean management at lower levels became presidents of companies. To be sure, there is no such thing as a ready-made Lean leader. Lean must be learned step-by-step, in each position held, as a person ascends the hierarchy of an organization.

Next, Mr. Person tells why executives resisted the introduction of Scientific Management:

> "The chief executive must necessarily present the proposition, to undertake the development of scientific

management, to his associate executives, as a systematic whole – as a doctrine and complete body of procedures – because he is presenting a matter of future policy. It must be so presented to them because they must become agents of its development, and as such they must comprehend it in advance in its entirety. The magnitude of the picture appalls them and stimulates the active emergence of every mental and temperamental objection. They see that it means the upsetting of a complex set of procedures to which they are accustomed: they envision the ultimate aggregate of changes in a single picture, without realizing that the changes will come about only gradually and their adjustments will have to be made only gradually." (pp. 433-434)

But why were workers more accepting of Scientific Management compared to executives?

"On the other hand it is usually presented to workers not as a doctrine, not as a complete system of which the details and consequences must be constructed in their imaginations, but, as successive small increments of procedure, one at a time, each of which is comprehensible, is demonstrated, proved out, and become familiar before the next is presented. Workers also by temperament and experience are more accustomed to respond to suggestions than are individualistic executives. In short, the executive group is difficult because scientific management must be presented to them as a philosophy, doctrine and inclusive system; the worker group is not difficult because the new methods are presented to it by increments each of which means a relatively small and comprehensible change." (p. 434)

This indicates that the presentation of Lean to executives has been, in many cases, wrong. Either it is presented incorrectly as tools or as a "manufacturing thing," or as so enormous a change that executives cannot follow it and quickly lose interest. It suggests that to gain wider acceptance for Lean management, its advocates should anticipate this specific negative reaction and be prepared to address it by providing detailed explanations of the "Continuous Improvement" principle and its practical application. Likewise, the "Respect for People" principle must be explained in detail and with many examples of its practical application. Once executives gain an accurate understanding of Lean management, the next step is to ensure that the leaders do not become lost in their Lean transformation [18].

Finally, failure to adjust to the feedback from executives could one day make Lean management go the way of Scientific Management. Indeed, academics and consultants recently began touting "innovation" as the next big thing after Lean.

Notes

[1] F.W. Taylor, *The Principles of Scientific Management*, Harper & Brothers Publishers, New York, NY, 1911, p. 115. In a nutshell, Scientific Management can be described as a system of production management that, if done correctly, resulted in a much more efficient batch-and-queue (push) production system; 2-3 times more efficient than basic batch-and-queue production. Its application was later extended to non-production activities and to non-manufacturing industries. Its main foci were "betterment" of the work and "cooperation" among the management and the workers. Some of its principles, methods, and tools are the same or similar to that found in Lean management.

[2] "The Toyota Way 2001," Toyota Motor Corporation, internal document, Toyota City, Japan, April 2001

[3] B. Emiliani, *REAL LEAN: Understanding the Lean Management System*, Volume One, The CLBM, LLC, Wethersfield, Conn., 2007,

[4] M.L. Emiliani, "Origins of Lean Management in America: The Role of Connecticut Businesses", *Journal of Management History*, Vol. 12, No. 2, pp. 167-184 2006, http://www.theclbm.com/articles/lean_in_conn.pdf

[5] See B. Emiliani, with D. Stec, L. Grasso, and J. Stodder, *Better Thinking, Better Results: Case Study and Analysis of an Enterprise-Wide Lean Transformation*, second edition, The CLBM, LLC, Wethersfield, Conn., 2007

[6] Harlow S. Person obtained a Ph.D. in economics from the University of Michigan in 1903.

[7] D. Wren, *The History of Management Thought*, fifth edition, John Wiley & Sons, Inc., New York, NY, 2005, p. 189

[8] "Taylor's Testimony Before the Special House Committee" in *Scientific Management: Comprising Shop Management, Principles of Scientific Management, Testimony Before the House Committee*, F.W. Taylor, with foreword by Harlow S. Person, Harper & Brothers Publishers, New York, NY, 1947, p. 43

[9] Reference [8], pp. 30, 62

[10] H.S Person in reference [8], p. xii

[11] E.H. Schell, *The Technique of Executive Control*, McGraw-Hill Book Company, Inc., New York, NY, 1924

[12] O. Tead, *The Art of Leadership*, McGraw-Hill Book Company, Inc., New York, NY, 1935

[13] "Leadership in Scientific Management," Harlow S. Person in *Scientific Management in American Industry*, The Taylor Society, Harper

and Brothers Publishers, New York, NY, 1929, pp. 427-439

[14] M.L. Emiliani, "Linking Leaders' Beliefs to Their Behaviors and Competencies," *Management Decision*, Vol. 41, No. 9, pp. 893-910, 2003

[15] M.L. Emiliani and D.J. Stec, "Using Value Stream Maps to Improve Leadership," *Leadership and Organizational Development Journal*, Vol. 25, No. 8, pp. 622-645, 2004

[16] M.L. Emiliani, "Lean Behaviors," *Management Decision*, Vol. 36, No. 9, pp. 615-631, 1998

[17] M.L. Emiliani, "Continuous Personal Improvement," *Journal of Workplace Learning*, Vol. 10, No. 1, pp. 29-38, 1998

[18] M.L. Emiliani and D.J. Stec, "Leaders Lost in Transformation," *Leadership and Organizational Development Journal*, Vol. 26, No. 5, pp. 370-387, 2005

3 Can Lean Exit the Tool Age?

Lean management advocates have recently begun concerted efforts to push Lean out of the tool age and help people understand Lean as a management system. This article examines what happened when the advocates of an earlier system of management, Scientific Management, sought to change the widely-held view that it was nothing more than a set of tools to improve efficiency. Knowledge of their efforts might help us succeed, provided Lean has not already suffered too much damage.

Scientific Management was the hot new industrial management practice starting in the late 1890s through the 1940s. But soon after the principles and practices of this new management system were codified in 1911 [1], most managers and observers started to interpret it as nothing more than a set of tools to improve labor efficiency. Other people saw it as a ruthless way to benefit corporations and their shareholders at the expense of workers. They also failed to acknowledge its long evolution in thinking and practice which corrected many of its deficiencies.

Almost immediately the advocates and foremost practitioners of Scientific Management were put on the defensive. It was so controversial that its principal architect, Frederick Winslow Taylor, was called to testify before a House Committee in 1912. Taylor had to explain to members of the committee that the management system he and others created was not evil, and went to great lengths to set the record straight over four days of testimony. He said [2]:

"Scientific management is not any efficiency device, not a device of any kind for securing efficiency; nor is it any bunch or group of efficiency devices. It is not a new system of figuring costs; it is not a new scheme of paying men; it is not a piecework system; it is not a bonus system; it is not a premium system; it is no scheme for paying men; it is not holding a stopwatch on a man and writing things down about him; it is not time study; it is not motion study nor an analysis of the movements of men; it is not the printing and ruling and unloading of a ton or two of blanks [office forms] on a set of men and saying, 'Here's your system go use it.' It is not divided foremanship or functional foreman- ship; it is not any of these devices which the average man calls to mind when scientific management is spo- ken of...what I am emphasizing is that these devices in whole or in part are not scientific management; they are useful adjuncts to scientific management, so are they also useful adjuncts of other systems of management."

In other words, do not mistake the tools and methods used for improvement as constituting the underlying philosophy of the Scientific Management system. Mr. Taylor goes on to say:

"Now, in its essence, scientific management involves a complete mental revolution on the part of the working- man... as to their duties towards their work, towards their fellow men, and toward their employers. And it involves the equally complete mental revolution on the part of those on the management's side... as to their duties toward their fellow workers in the management, toward their workmen, and toward all of their daily problems. And without this complete mental revolution [of cooperation] on both sides scientific management does not exist.... [this] constitutes the first step towards scientific management.

...[it is] their duty to cooperate in producing the largest possible surplus [of profits to share] and as to the necessity of substituting exact scientific knowledge for opinions or the old rule-of-thumb or individual knowledge. If the use of the system does not make both sides happier, then it is no good... Scientific management cannot exist in establishments with lions at the head of them... It ceases to be scientific management the moment it is used for bad."

Taylor is simply saying that zero-sum relations between laborers, between managers, and between labor and management are wasteful and will hinder industrial, economic, and human progress. Conventional management is zero-sum, while scientific management is not [3]. The mental revolution is the counterintuitive realization that non-zero-sum, mutually beneficial relations will yield better outcomes for everyone. If managers use Scientific Management to advance their own selfish zero-sum interests, then what they are doing can no longer be called Scientific Management. The tools won't be effective if zero-sum conditions exist. Just as we have seen with Lean, the tools are ineffective and lead to backslide if zero-sum conditions exist; for example, if the "Respect for People" principle is not in existence [4]. Likewise, we should say: "It ceases to be Lean management the moment it is used for bad." Lean will not exit the tool age if zero-sum conditions persist, which by its very nature demonstrates disrespect for people.

Taylor's testimony illustrates the depth of misunderstanding faced by the advocates and premier industrial practitioners of Scientific Management. They had the overwhelming task of convincing anyone who would listen that Scientific Management was a management system and not a set of tools to improve efficiency. By the late 1920s, Scientific Management had been around for about 25 years. So its practitioners and advocates started writing retrospective papers that discussed successes and failures. Harlow S. Person, (1875-1955) was a prominent advocate of Scientific Management since before 1910. He served as a managing director and later as president of The Taylor Society from the mid-1920s to the late 1940s, and thus had a unique perspective on the challenges that the movement faced over a four-decade period.

In 1929 Mr. Person contributed a paper titled "The Origin and Nature of Scientific Management" to the book *Scientific Management in American Industry* [5]. This paper contains valuable insights, both current to 1929 and in retrospect, with regards to where and how Scientific Management stumbled. Hopefully we can learn something from this to help Lean successfully emerge from the tool age, which Scientific Management was unable to do.

Mr. Person has many interesting observations including:

> "...[scientific management] must be based on a harmony of desires and understandings within the group. That is one reason why there are so few complete developments of scientific management, even though American industry generally has been profoundly influenced by its

spirit and has come to utilize practically all of its mechanisms. In the first place, managers are reluctant, except under the compulsion of circumstances, to undertake revolutionary improvement; in the second place, because of natural basic conditions of prosperity in America, there has not been general compulsion toward ideals and methods marking a radical departure from opportunism. The urge for a consistent and well-rounded development of scientific management, as distinguished from unconscious influence of its spirit and conscious appropriation of some of its waste-saving mechanisms, has been felt chiefly by those rare leaders who are naturally responsive to ideals of perfection in technical accomplishment and human relations." (p. 11)

The great majority of executives are more interested in micro-evolutionary department-specific improvement, rather than revolutionary improvement across the enterprise. And when business conditions are good, why bother doing anything new? Therefore, the use of efficiency improvement tools, which often reflects opportunism on the part of managers to secure short-term gains (i.e. "quick hits"), are what executives favor.

"Another reason is that generally the American executive does not take to doctrines, theories, or systems. He has lived in a period of opportunism, has been concerned chiefly with dynamic problems of frontier industry, and has been engaged in going things rather than in reading and thinking about things. Doctrines and systems do not excite his interests; in fact, a new doctrine or system is likely at first to invite rejection without serious consideration." (p. 11-12)

In general, tools excite executives, not management systems. This is what most Lean consultants have quickly figured out. There is gainful employment in teaching the tools, and mostly frustration and poor sales if one tries to teach the system. In addition, most executives are not fond of reading and thinking, but instead like to focus their attention on doing their daily routine. This places a major handicap on any new system of management.

Person continues:

> "In time, however, it is almost certain to have great influence if it has integrity and vigor, for the detailed beliefs or practices expressing a doctrine may be held or practiced by individuals who do not hold or are not informed concerning the doctrine as a whole." (p. 12)

Mr. Person thought that over time the Scientific Management system would diffuse and someday make up the fabric of executive thinking and management practice. He was wrong, at least so far.

> "A large number of plants dominated by tradition [of management practice] and imitation has naturally appropriated some of the mechanisms of scientific management, and although the net result has been a gradual rising of the level of management in such plants, this result has not been achieved in all cases. Very serious damage in individual instances to managerial effectiveness and harmonious relations with workers, and to the good repute of scientific management, has resulted from the failure to adopt ideals and

spirit along with mechanisms. It is in this class of plants that the superficial 'efficiency engineer' has found his clientele, and he has not hesitated to seek the advantage of proclaiming himself a representative of scientific management, the harm he has been able to bring temporarily to the repute of scientific management has been considerable." (p. 13)

In this passage Person is particularly critical of the "efficiency engineer" whose specialty is the tools, but who represents himself as a disciple of Scientific Management without full knowledge of the system. The equivalent of this today would be the kaizen consultant or Lean trainer, for example, whose specialty is the tools, but who represents himself as a disciple of Lean management without full knowledge of the system. In other words, they are experts at "Continuous Improvement," but lack deep knowledge of the "Respect for People" principle; and especially how the two principles function together [6,7].

"The concern of scientific management for harmonious industrial relations, and workers' prosperity and good-will, has always been deep, for one of the first discoveries of research in management is that good-will is a productive power independent of the efficiency of equipment and methods, and adds to the efficiency of equipment and methods. But scientific management considers workers' welfare and good-will, not as something detached which can be generated effectively as a thing apart from the spirit and methods of management, but as something which is a consequence of and integral with these. Good management and workers' wel-

fare are the two terms of an equation; it matters little
which term is put first. Scientific management aims...
to eliminate factors of the environment which are irri-
tating and the cause of frictions, and to promote common understandings, tolerances and the spirit of team
work." (pp. 16-17)

Unfortunately, there are too many executives who ignore
obvious cause-and-effect relationships when it comes to
improvement and the workers. Kaizen that leads to layoffs
creates ill-will and friction, undercuts teamwork, and destroys
worker's desire to participate in future improvement activities. Kaizen threatens their welfare; the cause-and-effect is
clear. But many executives choose to deny this reality, indicating that they do not want responsibility for the workers. If
that's the case, then should they be an executive? By these
actions, executives are doing all they can to make sure Lean
never exits the tool age.

Scientific Management ended its run a few years after World
War II, in large part because executives failed to understand
it as a system and did not comprehend its true meaning; a
non-zero-sum management system.

Significant efforts were made over a four decade period to
help Scientific Management exit the tool age. The primary
change in tactic, which was initiated in the late 1920s, was to
view this as a leadership problem. The Scientific
Management community eagerly looked to social psychology, industrial psychology, and the emerging field of leadership studies for answers that could help them. But none came.
What does this foretell for Lean?

Some of the ideas and many tools of Scientific Management were picked up by Lean management, either directly or discovered separately. If Lean continues to be seen as a bunch of tools, then it is likely that its tools will be subsumed into the next big thing. Who knows what that will be or when it will come along, but one thing is certain: it will be a big waste because there is nothing fundamentally wrong with Lean management. It is a greatly improved non-zero-sum management system that explicitly incorporates the human dimension through the "Respect for People" principle – a feature that Scientific Management struggled with.

The Lean community helped create the problem of another management system becoming widely viewed as a set of tools. We should want to recover from this repeat error. The question is: How do we do it?

Taylor and Person identified three executive characteristics that they thought stood in the way of understanding Scientific Management as a management system:

- Zero-sum mindset
- Focused principally on doing things
- Satisfaction with the current state

These are three tough nuts to crack! They surely support Taylor's and Person's view that it was rare to find leaders who want to achieve something great, both technically and in human relations. The three nut problem also limits us today, and should be among the key areas that the Lean community focuses on in its presentation of Lean as a management system.

Finally, it won't do much good for Lean to exit the tool age if the current generation of managers understands Lean as a management system but is unwilling or unable to pass that knowledge and practice on to future generations of managers. We need to think about how to do that as well.

Notes

[1] F.W. Taylor, *The Principles of Scientific Management*, Harper & Brothers Publishers, New York, NY, 1911. In a nutshell, Scientific Management can be described as a system of production management that, if done correctly, resulted in a much more efficient batch-and-queue (push) production system; 2-3 times more efficient than basic batch-and-queue production. Its application was later extended to non-production activities and to non-manufacturing industries. Its main foci were "betterment" of the work and "cooperation." Some of its principles, methods, and tools are the same or similar to that found in Lean management.

[2] *Scientific Management: Comprising Shop Management, Principles of Scientific Management, Testimony Before the House Committee*, F.W. Taylor, with foreword by Harlow S. Person, Harper & Brothers Publishers, New York, NY, 1947, pp. 26-27, 30-31, 152, and 191

[3] Scientific Management was an early attempt to create a non-zero-sum management system. Technically, however, it retains zero-sum features because it is still a batch-and-queue (push) system. However, Scientific Management is much less zero-sum compared to simple batch-and-queue management thinking and practice. The rationale for improved human relations and the work analysis methods developed by the leaders of Scientific Management (or separately by others) were major advances in management thinking and practice.

[4] "The Toyota Way 2001," Toyota Motor Corporation, internal document, Toyota City, Japan, April 2001

[5] Harlow S. Person in *Scientific Management in American Industry*, Harlow S. Person, editor, The Taylor Society, Harper and Brothers Publishers, New York, NY, 1929, chapter 1, pp. 1-22

[6] B. Emiliani, *REAL LEAN: Understanding the Lean Management System,* Volume One, The CLBM, LLC, Wethersfield, Conn., 2007

[7] B. Emiliani, with D. Stec, L. Grasso, and J. Stodder, *Better Thinking, Better Results: Case Study and Analysis of an Enterprise-Wide Lean Transformation*, second edition, The CLBM, LLC, Wethersfield, Conn., 2007

4 How to Make Lean Last a Long Time

*Backslide is a major concern of people who are engaged in
Lean transformations. But do they understand its causes,
and are they applying the right countermeasures to prevent
it from happening to them? History confirms that doing
nothing will guarantee rapid deterioration of the management system when routine changes occur, such as hiring or
promoting new executives, or new company ownership.*

The threat of backslide looms large in every Lean transformation. It is a major concern because there is a very high
probability that backslide will occur, and nobody likes to see
their good ideas and dedicated efforts fade away. In addition,
when backslide happens many people will blame Lean and
say: "See, Lean doesn't work." That, of course, is not true.
But the discipline needed to keep Lean management alive and
in good health is more than most leaders can muster. And
there are special challenges for senior managers that typically go unanswered. A look back in time to the era when
Scientific Management was popular can clarify the causes of
backslide in Lean transformations and assist in identifying
practical countermeasures.

Scientific Management emerged from the machine age in the
late 1880s as the first purposefully designed system of industrial management [1]. Practiced correctly, it increases the efficiency of batch-and-queue (push) production systems two to
three times compared to simple batch-and-queue production.
Its application was soon extended to non-production activities
such as office work and to non-manufacturing businesses

such as higher education.

The focus of Scientific Management was "betterment" of the work and "cooperation" between management and the workers. Some of its principles, methods, and tools are the same or similar to that found in Lean management. But let's be clear, Scientific Management is not Lean management. It is an important branch along the evolutionary path to Lean.

Economist Horace B. Drury wrote a book in 1915 titled: *Scientific Management: A History and Criticism* [2]. Drury's book contains telling retrospectives of the status of Scientific Management in several companies in which the system was introduced. It turns out that backslide was a big concern then just as it is now for Lean. For example:

> "At the birthplace of scientific management [the Midvale Steel Company], and the seat of its development from 1882 to 1889, the system is said to have remained static since Frederick W. Taylor left in the latter year... Midvale has adopted none of the later features which have made the old scientific management seem but fragmentary." (p. 154)

In other words, the main proponent of Scientific Management left the company and no manager advanced it further. Thus, the system fell into disrepair by virtue of it having remained static post-1889, while Scientific Management continued to evolve. Another example:

> "... the system installed there [at the Bethlehem Steel Company] met with disapproval of Charles M. Schwab

[president of Bethlehem Steel] when he came into control of the plant about September, 1901... The present owners say that they have rid themselves of Taylor and his ideas, and declare in their irritation that they 'don't want to hear anything more about scientific management.' Mr. Schwab continued to debase scientific management's better ideas regarding the treatment of workers... Though Schwab is thus alleged to have wandered away from certain of the teachings of scientific management, it is claimed that on the whole his plant has retained the important features of the system. Thus we meet with conflicting testimony: that of the Bethlehem management that Taylor and his system have been 'kicked out', and that of some of the opposing party, who have revisited the works, and say that its essentials are in operation." (pp. 154-156)

In this passage we learn that the best practitioners of Scientific Management viewed Bethlehem Steel's efforts to have faltered after Taylor left, while the management and other parties, who most likely could not tell the difference between genuine and fake Scientific Management, maintained that the system was still in place. We see the same thing today. In companies where Fake Lean has won out over REAL Lean, Lean management is said by some to still be in place.

While this outcome is unfortunate it is important to recognize that new leaders, such as Mr. Schwab, made decisions that were sensible from their point of view. In most cases, they are simply doing what they were trained to do and what they thought was best for the company and its shareholders. Nevertheless, this illustrates how disruptive changes in executives or company ownership can be to the new management system. The lost opportunities will be enormous.

Drury cites the work of Harrington Emerson, a noted "efficiency engineer" who in the early 1900s worked with various railroad companies to improve railway operations and locomotive maintenance [3]:

> "Since [Harrington] Emerson's connection with the Santa Fe [Railroad] was severed, there have been those who have said that the value of the work was illusory, and that now, as a matter of fact, the entire structure has been torn down by the officers of the company." (p. 162)

Drury, quoting Emerson, says this was due to:

> "…a change in vice-presidents, two changes in superintendents of motive power, and not one of my original group of assistants is left." (p. 163)

Again, when key people leave, particularly executives, the system begins to deteriorate.

Drury goes on to say:

> "We may conclude that, while the facts do not warrant our saying with some that all of the stock illustrations of scientific management are to-day practically nonexistent, nevertheless it is true that in each case something has happened to dim the glory of the achievement. Though abandoned but in a few cases, and convicted of failure in none, stagnation, disavowal, or

transformation, have destroyed their character as satisfactory evidence." (p. 164).

Drury notes that the early examples of the application of Scientific Management were experiments whose importance was not so great because the system had evolved and improved, particularly with regards to the attitude and practice of "cooperation" between management and the workers.

What matters more, according to Drury, are contemporary examples (circa 1905-1915) of the application of Scientific Management. He cites the following companies that installed improved forms of the Scientific Management system: The Tabor Manufacturing Company, Philadelphia, Pa; The Link-Belt Company, Philadelphia, Pa. facility; The Watertown Arsenal, Watertown, Mass.; The H.H. Franklin Manufacturing Company, Syracuse, N.Y.; [4], and The Joseph & Feiss Company; Cleveland, OH. Of these five organizations, only Link-Belt is operating today. Interestingly, Link-Belt characterizes Lean narrowly as a "manufacturing philosophy" and hence refers to it as "Lean manufacturing" [5]. Joseph & Feiss survives today as a non-U.S. made brand of clothing and accessories sold by Men's Wearhouse®.

Drury provides another example of backslide:

> "During the war [World War I] there were changes in personnel, including the withdrawal of Mr. Babcock [production manager at Franklin Manufacturing], and many of the features of scientific management which Mr. Babcock had highly developed fell into disuse." (p. 180)

Once again, the loss of key personnel severely disrupts the management system. Drury then discusses how, in most plants, Scientific Management has been installed only partially.

> "...Emerson tells us that in no plant has he had an opportunity to install his system as thoroughly as Taylor's ideas have been incorporated in the Tabor shop." (p. 186-187)

Drury, quoting Emerson, says:

> "In many plants our engagement was for very short periods. A limited sum [of money] would be appropriated with instructions to do the best we could in three months or six months." (p. 187)

Drury continues:

> "And so, to a large extent, has it been almost everywhere. Not only has the system been modified and minimized to meet financial limitations, but usually peculiar obstacles of one sort or another have affected the nature of the introduction. Thus, complete reorganization on efficiency lines are not very numerous, and pure scientific management is extremely rare... Perhaps they do not completely understand scientific management, but they have read Taylor's books, or Emerson's, or caught their spirit, – and one or another of the principles is adopted." (p. 187)

This passage should sound familiar to anyone who has tried to implement Lean. Today, one might say: "Perhaps they do not completely understand Lean management, but they have read Ohno's books, or Womack's, or caught their spirit, – and one or another of the principles is adopted."

Drury then seeks to answer the question: Which parts of Scientific Management were most sought after by managers?

> "...the aspect of the system of which this device is the central feature [time study and standardization] has been the most largely productive of all." (p. 196)

Thus, managers' central focus was rapid productivity improvement because it was the most profitable to them. Much like today, implementation of Lean is focused on the application of tools to quickly improve productivity. Executives who do this miss the big picture as well as more valuable opportunities.

Drury makes this interesting comment:

> "If the [scientific management] system were carried to its logical limits, the highest official [in a company] would become subordinate to others with respect to certain details of his conduct; while the humblest worker might quite properly be given a real authority in his own particular field." (p. 205)

This passage predicted what we would later see in organizations that correctly practice Lean management [6,7]. Drury had something else to say about the future:

> "But fifty years from now [c. 1965], when Taylor, Gantt, Barth, Cooke, Dodge, and the others will have been fol-

lowed by men who know not the kindly spirit of these pioneers, when shop management is once again regarded only as a money-making proposition, and when the new men look about them to see whether Taylor was right in saying that making money and harmony and human welfare [well-being] are not incongruous, what then will be the situation?" (p. 249)

It will pretty much be as we have it today; a situation where business is typically viewed narrowly as a zero-sum money-making machine, which will do nothing to make Lean last a long time. In fact, it could hasten its demise as executives search for "the next big thing" that will help them make money more easily than Lean will. Unfortunately, they will miss Lean management's greatest lessons with regards to thinking and learning.

Drury notes how Scientific Management helps change manager's fundamental approach to wealth creation:

"Scientific management is... significant because it is teaching the world a new way of gathering wealth. In the past the way to become rich has too often been that of exploiting one's fellows. But under scientific management... one notes a shifting of emphasis towards efforts to increase *total* wealth." (p. 254)

In other words, a shift from zero-sum to non-zero-sum [8] thinking and management practice. That's what Scientific Management tried to teach managers then, and that's what Lean management tries to teach managers now. But the lesson cannot be learned if Lean is seen by executives as nothing more that a set of tools to improve productivity and achieve some "quick wins." What they fail to see are the "quick losses" that also accrue from misapplication of the Lean management system.

Annual surveys conducted by the Lean Enterprise Institute consistently show that backslide is among the top three obstacles for implementing Lean [9]. And it should be, given what people have experienced decades before us when they tried to implement a new management system.

To avoid backslide and achieve long-term prosperity, a company has to maintain continuity in Lean management practice. An executive who learns Lean very well and finally becomes a non-zero-sum wealth creator will eventually move on. The board of directors, not having a proper understanding of Lean, will usually, and inadvertently, replace the executive with a zero-sum wealth destroyer [10]. Then, after a period of time where one or more zero-sum wealth destroyers occupy key offices, a new non-zero-sum wealth creator is brought in to turn the company around. Cycling thorough executives in this manner is waste, so is the perpetual need for re-training of top leaders.

Executives who "get it" are rare because it runs against their normal zero-sum conception of wealth creation [11]. Most executives view zero-sum as capitalism, and non-zero-sum as socialism – simple as that. It is difficult to overcome the biases, stereotypes, and fallacious arguments against non-zero-sum ways of doing business. The negative political, economic, legal, and social characterizations made by theorists over the last one hundred years have been very effective at undercutting clear and pragmatic business thinking.

People who understand Lean management will see zero-sum business as capitalism with a small brain; one that does not think of cause-and-effect and is thus inconsistent with the "Respect for People" principle [12,13]. Arrogance, also known as "big company disease," helps keep problems hidden, so zero-sum outcomes remain out of sight and therefore go uncorrected. Managerial self-interest and zero-sum thinking, whose effects are detrimental to a business and its key stakeholders, are what Frederick W. Taylor and others that followed had labored unsuccessfully to correct [14]. So far, Lean management, which is capitalism with a big brain, is not faring much better.

This is due in part to the fact that managers typically see business as a "game" or a "battle," which creates or perpetuates an incorrect view that business is a zero-sum activity just as sports games or military battles are. The many problems that result from zero-sum thinking make it much more difficult to manage a business. This helps explain why executives persistently claim there is a shortage of qualified leaders, which absolutely cannot be the case since anyone can create a wasteful current state. Managers obviously need to be taught that business is not defined as, nor does it need to be operated as, a zero-sum "game" or "battle."

It is no surprise that both Scientific Management and Lean management have prospered in smaller companies or in individual plant sites of large corporations [15]. Executives can more clearly see the effects of zero-sum thinking, and many likely were also victims of zero-sum thinking by their customers or suppliers. Therefore, they are less interested in zero-sum thinking. The advantages of Lean management should be much greater in large organizations because they are usually inefficient, but rooting out zero-sum thinking can appear to be an overwhelming challenge. It would probably be difficult to find more than a handful of Fortune 500 CEOs who would admit to possessing a fundamentally flawed view of wealth creation [16].

Increasing total wealth shouldn't be so hard to do, regardless of the size or type of business, but it is. However, there are things that can be done to improve the situation, assuming that executives are truly serious about improvement, wealth creation, and the long-term viability of the business. Some practical countermeasures that can be applied to perpetuate REAL Lean management over generations of executives include:

- Get proper Lean management system training and practice daily on-the-job
- Promote only those people who are very good at understanding and practicing both "Continuous Improvement" and "Respect for People"
- Develop a deep internal bench for executive succession
- Make it a board-level responsibility to help perpetuate Lean management

The high risk of backslide can be reduced if executives will do some relatively simple things in a consistent fashion over time. This will help protect and nurture investments of time, people, and money made in Lean transformations.

Notes

[1] F.W. Taylor, *The Principles of Scientific Management*, Harper & Brothers Publishers, New York, NY, 1911

[2] H.B. Drury, *Scientific Management: A History and Criticism*, third edition, Studies in History, Economics and Public Law, the Faculty of Political Science of Columbia University, Columbia University Press, 1922, republished by AMS Press, Inc., New York, NY, 1968

[3] H. Emerson, *Twelve Principles of Efficiency*, The Engineering Magazine Company, New York, NY, 1913

[4] See G. Babcock, *The Taylor System in Franklin Management*, The Engineering Magazine Company, New York, NY, 1918. or http://en.wikipedia.org/wiki/Franklin_%28automobile%29.

[5] Link-Belt Construction Equipment Company web site, http://www.linkbelt.com/linkbelt/about/frameabout.htm

[6] J. Liker, *The Toyota Way*, McGraw-Hill, New York, NY, 2004

[7] B. Emiliani, with D. Stec, L. Grasso, and J. Stodder, *Better Thinking, Better Results: Case Study and Analysis of an Enterprise-Wide Lean Transformation*, second edition, The CLBM, LLC, Wethersfield, Conn., 2007

[8] For additional explanation of zero-sum, see http://en.wikipedia.org/wiki/Zero-sum

[9] The Lean Enterprise Institute's survey results can be found at http://www.lean.org/Community/Registered/SurveyResultsList.cfm

[10] By definition these types of executives are wealth destroying because they are unaware of waste, unevenness, and unreasonableness. They are typically results-focused to a fault, and resort to artificial means to create wealth (or the appearance of wealth) using short-term methods such as those listed in Note [16].

[11] Not to be confused with the common practice of maximizing shareholder value, principally short-term, for the benefit of investors at the expense of other stakeholders such as employees, suppliers, customers, and communities. Doing this typically causes tremendous damage. Executives clearly have a responsibility to *create* shareholder value, but they quickly run into problems when they seek to *maximize* shareholder value.

[12] "*The Toyota Way 2001*," Toyota Motor Corporation, internal document, Toyota City, Japan, April 2001

[13] B. Emiliani, *REAL LEAN: Understanding the Lean Management System*, Volume One, The CLBM, LLC, Wethersfield, Conn., 2007

[14] See "An Institutional Reconstruction of Scientific Management: On

the Lost Theoretical Logic of Taylorism," S. Wagner-Tsukamoto, *Academy of Management Review*, Vol. 32, No. 1, pp. 105-117, 2007 and "Testimony Before the Special House Committee" in *Scientific Management: Comprising Shop Management, Principles of Scientific Management, Testimony Before the Special House Committee*, F.W. Taylor, foreword by Harlow S. Person, Harper & Brothers Publishers, New York, N.Y., 1947.

[15] For evidence of this, see the past winners of The Shingo Prize for businesses: http://www.shingoprize.org/Recipients/BusPrize/current.htm

[16] This flawed view can be found in the zero-sum techniques commonly used by executives to create wealth, which include: layoffs, cutting benefits, squeezing suppliers, delaying payments to suppliers, delivering poor quality products to customers, channel stuffing, insider trading, inflating earnings, plant and office closings, and price fixing, to name just a few. See "Improving Management Education" by M.L. Emiliani, *Quality Assurance in Education*, Vol. 14, No. 4, pp. 363-384, 2006

5 Manage to the Market

To a surprising extent, most businesses are managed as if they serve sellers' markets when in reality they serve buyers' markets. Managers often fail to recognize this inconsistency or how deeply it runs through their business. As a result, they continue to manage the business using mindsets, metrics, and systems designed to serve sellers markets. If you serve buyers' markets, then you should use the management system that is most responsive to that market. There isn't much in the way of choices; it's Lean management.

If you start a business, you're likely to begin satisfying customer demand using the batch-and-queue method in large part because it will seem to make the most sense. Managers raised in this tradition operate with the mindset that customer's orders will be completed when it is convenient and cost-effective for the company to do it. This quickly becomes the prevailing habit and pervades how all work gets done.

Over time rigid cost accounting systems, policies and procedures, implicit rules, and decision-making establish organizational routines that support batch-and-queue systems and mindset. Additional investments will be made over the years to further develop and refine these features, which will simply reinforce and legitimize the current way of thinking and working. New people hired into this system soon come to think that it is a good way to do business and get work done. After all, if there were better ways to do things, they would be in use.

Unfortunately, the executives have fallen into a massive trap that they can not easily get out of. That is, they've grown their business using a system of management that was designed to serve sellers' markets. The executives put into place a producer-focused system of management, not a customer-focused system of management. As a result, customers have to wait for the product or service, pay higher prices, and contend with poor quality. Their tolerance for that won't last forever.

Invariably, circumstances change and so do customers, and the carefully-crafted producer focused management system, which was once a great asset, now becomes an even greater liability as customers realize they have alternatives. Executive ego, sunk costs, and deep-rooted bias toward maintaining the status quo make it very difficult for management to lead and make the necessary system-wide changes. This is why most brownfield businesses are unable to successfully transform from producer-focused sellers' market to customer-focused buyers' market.

Most businesses operate in buyers' markets, which mean there is lots of competition and customers have many sources of supply to consider. Thus, we have to listen to customers if we want the business to prosper. Strangely enough while most executives will tell you, without hesitation, their company serves buyers' markets, they manage their business, in almost every way, as if they serve sellers' markets. They fail to see how deeply batch-and-queue is embedded in their thinking, metrics, and business practices, and how these affect strategy and day-to-day management. Deep down, they don't feel they have to listen to customers and can instead do what they want. But of course they risk stumbling or even failing as a business.

In the automotive industry, clear examples of companies that operate in recognition of the fact that they serve buyers' markets are Toyota [1] and Honda. Examples of companies that operate as if they serve sellers' markets are General Motors, Ford, and Chrysler. Guess who has consistently prospered over time and who has not? In almost every competitive industry, you can think of examples of laggard businesses whose system of management is clearly misaligned with buyers' markets, while the leading performers are much better aligned with the actual markets they serve.

It is simple human nature to want sellers' markets. If we're honest, we'll all admit that we'd prefer to dominate the market or, better yet, have a monopoly. Why? Because it is easier. It is less work for management, it requires much less knowledge and fewer skills, we can manage from the office, it feeds our ego that we are smart and know what customers want, and it puts us in control – we like that a lot. A buyers' market means you have to think a lot more and work harder.

The United States consumer market was a sellers' market through the nineteenth century; everything that could be made was sold. This was called a "deficit economy." But the post 1890s machine age enabled inexpensive mass production which facilitated a transition to a "surplus economy." Thus, shortages became much less common starting around 1910. If your company failed to make this adjustment, you either sold your business for a low price or went out of business.

Interestingly, the roots of standard cost accounting dates back to the early mass production sellers' market era, circa 1860-1880. Complete standard cost systems were established around 1915 [2] and have remained with us to this day.

Indeed, absorption accounting is a key feature of batch-and-queue systems, and is required by the Financial Standards Accounting Board and in corporate financial reporting to the Internal Revenue Service. Thus, corporate performance measurement is rooted in the thinking associated with sellers' markets. The metrics contained in this accounting system are but a few of the many which companies use that fit better with sellers' markets. These do not serve management or customers well because they distort reality, lead to poor decisions, and delay or prevent change.

In 1886, Henry Towne, president of Yale and Towne Manufacturing Company, presented a paper at a meeting of the American Society of Mechanical Engineers in which he advocated formal study of the management of industrial organizations [3]. About the same time, Frederick W. Taylor was studying and experimenting with new practical ways to manage industrial organizations and improve productivity through the use of time studies, standardization, and incentive wage systems [4,5]. His work culminated in the 1911 publication of the book, *The Principles of Scientific Management* [6], and is best explained in the testimony Taylor gave to Congress in 1912 [7].

Taylor's interest was the elimination of waste, to simplify work and make it less strenuous, improve working conditions, increase worker pay when output was increased, and improve company and national competitiveness. He didn't appear to have any interest in the type of market that a company served.

In 1890 the Sherman Antitrust Act was passed by Congress to prevent restraint of trade and monopolistic practices by large corporations [8]. Later, in 1914 Congress passed the Clayton Antitrust Act to outlaw monopolies and anti-competitive behavior as it affects consumers, such as increasing prices by purposefully limiting supply [9]. These Acts, in addition to other developments such as new machinery, more competitors, and falling prices meant that managers had to start doing a better job of tracking and managing and costs, internal transactions, output, etc.

Simple batch-and-queue production was ill-suited to the changing marketplace. Other people would recognize that the Scientific Management system, a more efficient form of batch-and-queue production, could be very helpful to managers struggling to cope with the emergence of buyers' markets and falling prices. This included industrialists such as John Mapes Dodge, Henry Dennison, and Henry Towne; economists and lawyers such as Stuart Chase and Louis Brandeis; government officials such as Herbert Hoover; and university educators such as Dexter Kimball, Harlow Person, and Edwin Gay. In 1922, Harlow Person said the following about managing to the market [10]:

> "On a sellers' market the conduct of a business is easy and management is simple – in fact, there does not have to be any real management. But now that you appear to be fact to face with a buyers' market and the necessity of developing real management, if you are to be successful in a most intense competition, if your competitor, instead of yourself, is to be the one to disappear in some readjustment of productive capacity to consumer demand, it is expedient for you to inquire into the nature of that real management [Scientific

Management]... 'the customer is king'...we forget the
source of the impulse [for industrial activity] and come
to believe that it starts with the producer."

Zoom forward to the present-day and think about what current state value stream maps tell us, beyond how we have
been trained to interpret them. They depict the easiest and
most convenient way to do business. Simply put it is a type of
management that requires the lowest level of executive
knowledge and skill. It serves managements interests well,
but does not serve customers' interests. The batch-and-queue
processing shown in current state value stream maps is another way of saying to customers: "We're not listening to you;
we are doing what we want to do." How very revealing.

Most executives who profess to be practicing Lean are actually practicing more efficient forms of batch-and-queue – that
is to say, Fake Lean. This is obviously inconsistent with the
"Respect for People" principle [11,12], where people are customers, employees, suppliers, investors, and communities.
Their continuous improvement efforts will not succeed and
management will make many repeat errors driven by their
deep-rooted zero-sum view of business.

In contrast, future state value stream maps that have been
implemented depict a management possessing a much higher
level of knowledge and skills which better serves customer's
interests, and eventually management's interests as well. The
Lean material and information processing shown in future
state value stream maps is another way of saying to customers: "We are listening to you and we are doing what you
want us to do" [13]. This too is very revealing and also con-

sistent with the "Respect for People" principle.

How smart is it for executives to manage as if they are serving sellers' markets when in fact they are serving buyers' markets? It's not smart at all because it denies reality. It is always harder to manage a business when reality is ignored, and it creates unacceptable risks. What we have in Lean is a system of management that is much more responsive to dynamic buyers' markets, and includes a safeguard of "Respect for People" to make sure executives do not unfairly take advantage of their position relative to any of the key stakeholders. If you serve buyers' markets, you should use the management system that is most responsive to that market.

But what about the case when some product lines feed buyers' markets, while other product lines contain proprietary innovations or are protected by patents or trademarks, and thus managed in the style typical of a static sellers' market? Having an advantage is wonderful, but be careful. Sellers' markets do not last forever. Customers will remember that you overcharged them, made them wait too long, or gave them quality problems, and many will defect to competitors when the opportunity to do so arises. In general executives should seek to manage the business in ways that improve responsiveness to changing market conditions; rather than focus on fortifying a stronghold, milking a few cash cows for five or ten years, or eliminating the competition, none of which prepare them for the day when they will have to face a buyers' market. They will be without the needed knowledge, skills, and capabilities to prosper when things change.

Mistaking buyers' markets for sellers' markets is a common

management error. It reflects management's tolerance for errors and a lack of interest in root cause analysis. Imagine an engineer who designed a bridge that kept falling down. We would consider such an engineer to be poorly educated and bad at doing their job. Mistaking buyers' markets for sellers' markets on an ongoing basis will eventually lead to serious financial and non-financial problems, akin to the engineer's bridge that keeps falling down. Managers make lots of errors, but rarely are the root causes ever identified, so one can expect such failures to occur again in the future.

So what have we learned? Three things; first that managing as if a company serves sellers' markets when it in fact serves buyers' markets is not a smart thing to do because it denies reality. Second, Lean is a better management system for serving buyers' markets, but Fake Lean won't get you there, only REAL Lean will. And third, executives who adopt Lean to help perpetuate a false sellers' market ignore the "Respect for People" principle. That will eventually hurt the business and its key stakeholders.

You may ask, "What should I do?" You can start by accepting the reality of your markets and also make sure you do not unfairly exploit your advantages in the sellers' markets that you serve. It would also help to gain a correct understanding of Lean as a management system and all of its wonderful nuances and inter-connections, and practice REAL Lean every day. Finally, be sure to establish a plan for long-term continuity in Lean management practice.

One last thing to consider; executives represent a market for business improvement methods, and tools are typically what these executive customers want. Tools represent small advances to the current system of management, which is typically zero-sum batch-and-queue. Tools have great appeal because they can help executives get the zero-sum job done better. Tools go hand-in-hand with the management attitude "We're in a sellers' market", even if the company really is not. Tools are appealing to executives because it helps give the appearance that they are being proactive and doing something useful.

However, tools have a big downside; they also help managers avoid the deep and wide changes needed to serve their buyers' markets. For decades, Lean management has been portrayed as "tools for the manager's tool kit." Some people unwittingly helped create that perception, and many others gladly fed that perception. But the result thus far is clear; most businesses that have adopted Lean are still operating a zero-sum batch-and-queue management system and thus perpetuating management's sellers' market attitude. Sometimes responding to customer pull can backfire and perpetuate "me first" attitude, versus creating the desired "customer first" attitude and practice among company executives [14].

Notes

[1] Taiichi Ohno, creator of Toyota's production system, was well aware of the shift from sellers' to buyers' markets. In 1978 he said: "The world has already changed from a time when industry could sell everything it produced to an affluent society where material needs are routinely met... We are now unable to sell our products unless we think ourselves into the very hears of our customers, each of whom has different concepts and tastes." Source: T. Ohno, *Toyota Production System*, Productivity Press, Portland, OR, 1988, p. xiv

[2] See *Manufacturing Costs and Accounts*, A.H. Church, McGraw-Hill Book Company, Inc., New York, NY, 1917 and *The Evolution of Cost Accounting to 1925*, S.P. Garner, The University of Alabama Press, 1954.

[3] H.R. Towne, "The Engineer as an Economist," *Transactions of The American Society of Mechanical Engineers*, Vol. 7, 1886, pp. 428-432.

[4] F.W. Taylor, "A Piece Rate System: Being a Step Toward Partial Solution of the Labor Question," *Transactions of The American Society of Mechanical Engineers*, Vol. 16, 1895, pp. 856-903

[5] F.W. Taylor, "Shop Management," *Transactions of The American Society of Mechanical Engineers*, Vol. 25, 1903, pp. 1337-1480

[6] F.W. Taylor, *The Principles of Scientific Management*, Harper & Brothers Publishers, New York, NY, 1911

[7] "Testimony Before the Special House Committee" in *Scientific Management: Comprising Shop Management, Principles of Scientific Management, Testimony Before the House Committee*, F.W. Taylor, with foreword by Harlow S. Person, Harper & Brothers Publishers, New York, NY, 1947

[8] See http://en.wikipedia.org/wiki/Sherman_Antitrust

[9] See http://en.wikipedia.org/wiki/Clayton_Antitrust_Act

[10] H.S. Person, "Shaping Your Management to Meet Developing Industrial Conditions," *Bulletin of the Taylor Society*, Vol. 7., No., 6, December 1922, re-published in *Scientific Management Since Taylor: A Collection of Authoritative Papers*, E.E. Hunt, editor, McGraw-Hill, 1924, reissued in 1972 by Hive Publishing Co., Easton, PA, pp. 125-126.

[11] "The Toyota Way 2001," Toyota Motor Corporation, internal document, Toyota City, Japan, April 2001

[12] B. Emiliani, *REAL LEAN: Understanding the Lean Management System,* Volume One, The CLBM, LLC, Wethersfield, Conn., 2007

[13] The customer-first message was clearly delivered in the first kaizen training seminars offered in the United States. M. Imai, "Introduction to

Kaizen," Kaizen Institute of America seminar at The Hartford Graduate Center, Hartford, Conn., May 9, 1988

[14] Standardized work for executives could help improve this situation. See M.L. Emiliani, "Standardized Work for Executive Leadership," *Leadership and Organizational Development Journal*, Vol. 29, No. 1, pp. 24-46, 2008

6 "We're Beyond That"

*Whether a company is new to Lean or has been practicing
Lean for ten years, it is common to hear executives say
"We're beyond that" when it comes to various aspects of
Lean management. Is it possible that they could really be
"beyond that"? A closer look reveals that executives who
say "We're beyond that" unknowingly undercut
continuous improvement and will be inconsistent
with the "Respect for People" principle.*

When explaining various aspects of Lean management to
executives it is common to hear them say: "We're beyond
that." It is an odd thing to say because it presumes a level of
mastery of Lean management which nobody can truly possess.
It shows extreme overconfidence, misunderstanding of what
Lean management really is, mislabeling non-Lean activities as
Lean, or perhaps gamesmanship. Can anyone who truly
believes in continuous improvement ever be "beyond that?"

What about executives who respond to surveys asking them
how far along their company is in its Lean transformation? It is
not unusual for them to rank their company six, seven, or eight
on a one-to-ten scale, after practicing Lean for only five or six
years, and mostly incorrectly at that! Not even Toyota would
rank itself that high. Again, it shows extreme overconfidence,
misunderstanding of what Lean management really is, mislabeling non-Lean activities as Lean, or perhaps gamesmanship.

Before we examine if anyone can really be "beyond that"
when it comes to Lean management, let's first see if we're

"beyond that" when it comes to the late nineteenth and early twentieth century management principles of an earlier management system, Scientific Management. Frederick Winslow Taylor's four principles of Scientific Management are [1]:

- Science, not rule of thumb
- Scientific selection of workers
- Scientific education and development of workers
- Cooperation between management and workers

Science, not rule of thumb
This principle addresses management's strong tendency to apply rule-of-thumb rather than understanding the details of the work that other people perform, or their own work activities and decision-making processes. The concern is that a casual attitude about management, unaware of cause-and-effect relationships, will eventually lead to ruin. It certainly can.

Top executives make a lot of errors. Some common errors include:

- Expense and revenue recognition
- Hiding debt
- Channel stuffing
- Insider trading
- Predatory pricing
- False advertising
- Defective goods or services
- Bid rigging
- Delaying payment to suppliers
- Unpaid labor
- Overcharging customers
- Bad strategy

When senior managers really mess things up what do they do? Root cause analysis? No, they typically use their employees, suppliers, and physical assets to subsidize and pay for their errors. Hmmm, sounds like rule-of-thumb corrective action to me. Laying people off, closing plants or office, and squeezing suppliers is the commonly accepted simple remedy to corporate financial problems, even when the problems are minor. There's no science in that.

So it looks like we're not "beyond that" when it comes to Taylor's first principle.

Scientific selection of workers

This principle addresses management's strong tendency to simply hire bodies when there is a lot of work to do. Practically anyone will suffice as long as they look alert and have a body temperature of 98.6 degrees.

Many of us have worked in companies that had poor hiring processes which result in people being hired who were not at all suited for the job. This causes a lot of extra work and headache for supervisors and managers who must try to make the best of poor hiring decisions. In addition senior managers commonly complain that they do not have the right people to get the job done or achieve the company's strategic objectives. So what do they do?

They typically seek to hire better people without really knowing what "better" means or what to look for. The common proxy for better people is to hire graduates of top business or engineering schools, which bids up the price for labor and can worsen existing cost problems. Or, they will establish an edict to hire only graduates whose grade-point average is 3.6 or higher. Hmmm, sounds like rule-of-thumb corrective action to me. There's no science in that.

So it looks like we're not "beyond that" when it comes to Taylor's second principle.

By the way, this situation can lead to even worse results. When the time comes to cut heads, it's usually lower-level people who are let go while the superstar new-hires are retained because they are judged to be more valuable. Often, the superstars have strong book knowledge but lack the practical knowledge to help the business succeed long-term. Thus, the people with the practical knowledge to run the business and who create value are gone, while those left behind may do more harm to the business – likely through the application of an increasing array of short-term zero-sum actions which in turn lead to the problems listed previously. Rule-of-thumb certainly can ruin a business.

If management did a root cause analysis of this problem – some science – they'd find that they do not understand business processes or the details of the work that must be done. They also do not understand who is better suited for this work or that, or how to cross-train people to take advantage of people's evolution in knowledge and work interests.

Toyota is well-known for its efforts to understand the work that needs to be done, determining who is better suited for the work, and how to cross-train people. And they apply this knowledge towards the development of well-thought out process for hiring people. Thus, they avoid hiring the wrong people most of the time.

Scientific education and development of workers

This principle addresses management's strong tendency to ignore or poorly manage the education and development of workers [2]. The issue today is not that education and development of workers is ignored, though that may be the case in some companies. Instead, these opportunities have become widely available, particularly in large corporations. However, management sometimes leaves it up to the workers and its educational services suppliers, typically with a small amount of input and oversight, to assume responsibility for learning activities and outcomes. While employees clearly benefit from such programs, the practical impact on the organization can be hard to discern.

Education is typically thought of as degree-seeking higher education. However, higher education is typically disconnected from actual workplace activities. Thus, people who graduate from expensive company-paid undergraduate and graduate programs often remain pigeon-holed in their current job. Or, the education may pay-off with a promotion, but they can't apply much of what they learned in school because it isn't the way their company does things.

Development is usually closely related to on-the-job activities, but it is often managed in such a way that workers and the company benefit only a little from these extensive efforts. Worse yet is when executives fail to make use of people who did well in development programs and thrived in their cross-training assignments, because they cling to the narrow view that functional specialists are better candidates for promotion.

Companies can end up with workers who earn three or four
master's degrees and have an impressive list of training and
development activities under their belt, but who make almost
no greater contribution to the business than they were doing
prior to receiving the graduate degrees and training.

Surely these outcomes are not universal and improvements
are being made. But they are common outcomes, and it tells
us that a lot of time and money has been wasted. Overall,
efforts to educate and develop workers typically lack rigor
and specific application to the workplace, and thus fall short
of desired outcomes for workers and the company.

In large measure, these education and development programs
are attempting to address the challenge of remaining competitive in the future. But the approach commonly taken is to
offer a large menu of programs and hope they will do some
good. Hmmm, sounds like rule-of-thumb corrective action to
me. There's no science in that.

So it looks like we're not "beyond that" when it comes to
Taylor's third principle.

There is one more thing to recognize. Notice how all of this
education and development has led to more rule-of-thumb
and less science.

In contrast, Toyota is also well-known for its efforts to educate
and develop workers to meet current and future challenges
[3,4,5]. This is done using a science or engineering basis, and
is also consistent with the "Respect for People" principle.

Cooperation between management and workers

This principle addresses management's strong tendency, sometimes intentional but mostly not, to foment uncooperative behavior between managers and workers. Zero-sum thinking is perceived by executives to be more business-like than non-zero-sum thinking, but it provokes uncooperative behaviors among affected stakeholders. The so-called "hard decisions" are usually those which merely trade one stakeholders' interest for another. So zero-sum decisions are not hard decisions as we have been led to believe. Rather, they are easy decisions; in fact the easiest decisions.

Along the same lines, workers bemoan management's consistent inability to "walk the talk." Saying one thing and doing another is an offshoot of zero-sum thinking. So is moving people around like chess-pieces, treating workers as if they are just a number, wasting their time on busy-work, blaming people for errors, playing favorites, or supporting organizational politics. These are but a few of the things that management does to reduce cooperation between managers and workers.

Look no further than the Detroit automotive industry for a zero-sum thinking stronghold. For decades they have relied on zero-sum power-based bargaining with employees, suppliers, and dealers. The effect of no or poor cooperation between management and workers often can't be input to a spreadsheet, but is sure is costly.

What do executives do to overcome this mindset? In most cases they do nothing because they see no need to abandon business-like zero-sum thinking. So there isn't even any rule-of-thumb corrective action.

Why do executives tend to think in zero-sum terms, even though business is not defined as such? Well, because it makes managing easier, not better just easier, at least that's how it appears to them. Also, they apparently think that zero-sum thinking is free; that it has no costs or perhaps they just don't care about the costs. They must also rationalize that zero-sum thinking adds value. But how can that be? The cost of poor cooperation is a non-issue if leaders believe the decisions they make are always correct.

What about those more humble executives who can sense there is a cost to conflicts among the key stakeholders; what do they do? They often conduct an employee survey, and a common finding is that there is poor communication. So the management team will typically hire consultants to help improve communication as a means of gaining cooperation. Hmmm, sounds like rule-of-thumb corrective action to me. There's no science in that because they have not bothered to understand the root causes of poor communication.

So it looks like we're not "beyond that" when it comes to Taylor's fourth principle.

It turns out we're having some difficulty getting beyond Taylor's four principles, now about one hundred years old. How, then, is it possible to say "We're beyond that" when it comes to Lean management? Well, you can say it, but that doesn't mean it's true.

First of all, Lean is widely understood as a "manufacturing thing" and not a system of management for the entire enterprise. So managers can't be "beyond that" if their fundamental understanding of Lean is incorrect. Do they fare any better with the principles of Lean management? The two overarching principles of Lean management are:

- Continuous Improvement
- Respect for People

Continuous Improvement

What is the common conception of continuous improvement? Generally, it is nothing more than tools for the manager's tool kit. Continuous improvement tools have typically been used to achieve short-term gains, with little understanding of how they can help improve the long-term position of the company. Since most executives don't see the connection between continuous improvement tools and processes to human learning, there is no way they can actually be "beyond that."

In addition, the tools are often used incorrectly. There is confusion between takt time and cycle time. The waste of "processing" is misunderstood by most people as "over-processing." Kaizen is referred to incorrectly as an "event." Standardized work is not established or not kept up-to-date. The list goes on.

Another way continuous improvement tools have been deployed in a zero-sum fashion is to require their use in manufacturing but nowhere else in the company. The non-manufacturing units are "free riders" because they enjoy the benefits of the manufacturing unit's improved performance without having to engage in continuous improvement efforts. This is clearly unfair and undercuts the "Respect for People" principle.

So it looks like we're not "beyond that" when it comes to the continuous improvement principle.

Respect for People

The "Respect for People" principle, if they are aware of it at all, is new to most executives, having been made explicit by Toyota Motor Corporation only recently as part of their expression of the "Toyota Way" [6]. Given that most managers are not "beyond that" for continuous improvement tools and processes, it is hard to believe they could be "beyond that" when it comes to the "Respect for People" principle. But that's what they say.

Since the continuous improvement tools have typically been deployed in a zero-sum fashion; such as process improvements that lead directly to layoffs, or suppliers are trained to use the tools so the buyer can quickly extract price concessions, the relationship between "Continuous Improvement" and "Respect for People" is clearly not understood.

Nor is "Respect for People" understood by executives at face value with regards to cooperation, or at deeper levels. For example, just think of all the bad performance metrics that workers have to deal with like earned hours and purchase price variance, which do nothing but create waste, unevenness, and unreasonableness. What about andon lights that are misused as way to blame people for quality or delivery problems and assess interdepartmental fines?

Not sharing the gains with key stakeholders, employees, suppliers, investors, customers, and communities, is also inconsistent with the "Respect for People" principle. Executives

who don't thoroughly understand the nuances and inter-connections in Lean management can't possibly be "beyond
that." The same was true for Scientific Management one hundred years ago.

Executives who are serious about learning won't say "We're
beyond that" because they know there is always more to
learn. Those who possess the "We're beyond that" attitude
unknowingly undercut continuous improvement. Further,
saying "We're beyond that" is also inconsistent with the
"Respect for People" principle because it reduces worker's
desire to learn more and try new things, which in turn short-
changes customers, investors, and suppliers.

Lean isn't the management system for executives who don't
want to learn.

Notes

[1] F.W. Taylor, *The Principles of Scientific Management*, Harper & Brothers Publishers, New York, NY, 1911

[2] Frederick Taylor gave an interesting explanation of scientific education and development of workers and its relationship to work standards, cooperation, teamwork, continuous improvement, and respect for people: He said: "...the modern surgeon. In his operations five or six men cooperate, each one doing in turn just what he should do. How does that finest mechanic teach his apprentices? Do you suppose that when the young surgeons come to their teachers, the skilled surgeons, they are told first of all: 'Now, boys, what we want first is your initiative; we want you to use your brains and originality to develop the best methods of doing surgical work. Of course you know we do have our own ways of performing these operations, but don't let that hamper you for one instant in your work. What we want is your originality and initiative. Of course you know, for example, when we are amputating a leg and come to the bone, we take a saw and cut the bone off. Don't let that disturb you for a minute; if you like it better, take an axe, take a hatchet, anything you please; what we want is your originality. What we want of all things is originality on your part.' Now that surgeon says to his apprentices just what we say to our apprentices under Scientific Management. He says: 'Not on your life. We want your originality, but we want you to invent upward not downward. We do not want any of your originality until you know the best method of doing work that we know, the best method that is now known to modern surgery. So you just get busy and learn the best method that is known to date under modern surgery; then, when you have got to the top by the present method, invent upward; then use your originality.' That is exactly what we say to our men. We say, 'We do not know the best; we are sure that in two or three years a better method will be developed than we know of; but what we know is the result of a long series of [scientific] experiments and careful study of every element connected with shop management; these standards that lie before you are the results of these studies. We ask you to learn how to use these standards as they are, and after that, the moment any man sees an improved standard, a better way of doing anything than we are doing, come to us with it; your suggestion will not only be welcome but we will join you in making a carefully tried experiment, which will satisfy both you and us and any other man that your improvement is or is not better than anything before. If that experiment shows that your method is better than ours, your method will become our method and every one of us will adopt that method until somebody gets a better one.'...If you allow each man to do his own way,

just exactly as he pleases, without any regard to science, science melts right away. You must have standards. We get some of our greatest improvements from the workmen in that way. The workmen, instead of holding back, are eager to make suggestions. When one is adopted it is named after the man who suggested it, and he is given a premium [financial reward] for having developed a new standard. So in that way we get the finest kind of team work, we have true cooperation, and our method, instead of inventing things that were out of date forty years ago, leads on always to something better than has been known before." From "The Principles of Scientific Management" by F.W. Taylor in *Scientific Management: First Conference at the Amos Tuck School Dartmouth College*, The Plimpton Press, Norwood, MA, 1912, pp. 53-55.

[3] S. Hino, *Inside the Mind of Toyota*, Productivity Press, New York, NY, 2006

[4] J. Liker, *The Toyota Way*, McGraw-Hill, New York, NY, 2004

[5] J. Liker and D. Meier, *Toyota Talent: Developing Your People the Toyota Way*, McGraw-Hill, New York, NY, 2007

[6] "The Toyota Way 2001," Toyota Motor Corporation, internal document, Toyota City, Japan, April 2001

7 Lean is Not a Theory

Many people have the mistaken impression that Lean management is a theory. The creators of Lean management would be disappointed, if not insulted, to learn that their real world system of management has come to be viewed as such. They were practical people who worked hard to understand the true nature of actual business problems and identify practical improvements, for the benefit of everyone.

It is always a surprise to learn that many people still consider Lean management to be theoretical. It's also strange to hear others say that Lean management came from academics in business or engineering schools, or from government agencies.

Related to this is the common confusion regarding what, exactly, is theory. People often say or imply that because they have not done something or are unfamiliar with something, it must be theory. Being unfamiliar with something or not having done something simply means you are not familiar with something or have not done something, nothing more.

Mistakes in perception are not desirable because they prevent people from learning more about things that could help them. Lean management is not a theory; it came from the real world, with zero contribution from any government and zero contribution from academics. So how did Lean come to be viewed as theory? Let's first understand what theory is.

Theory is defined as [1]:

"Systematically organized knowledge applicable in a

> wide variety of circumstances, esp. a system of assumptions, principles, and rules of procedure devised to analyze, predict, or otherwise explain the nature or behavior of specified phenomena."

The second dictionary definition of theory is: "Abstract reasoning, speculation." Most business people think of this definition when they think of theory. That's unfortunate because they immediately dismiss the possibility that there is anything practical that they could use. They should think of the first definition instead, which leads to many more possibilities.

What was Mr. Taiichi Ohno trying to do when he and his colleagues created Toyota's production system (TPS) [2]? Were they trying to develop a new theory? Not at all. They were trying to understand practical business problems and identify improvements [3]. Ohno said:

> "Above all, one of our most important purposes was increased productivity and reduced costs." (p. i)

The way he and his colleagues did this was by getting material and information to flow. Ohno goes on to say:

> "The technique we call the Toyota production system was born through our various efforts to catch up with the automotive industries of western advanced nations after the end of World War II, without the benefits of funds or splendid facilities." (p. i)

In other words, it was working people thinking about how to improve their day-to-day work.

"Our approach has been to investigate one by one the causes of various 'unnecessaries' in manufacturing operations and to devise methods for their solution, often by trial and error. The technique of kanban as a means of Just-in-time production, the idea and method of production smoothing, and Autonomation (Jidoka), etc., have all been created from such trial-and-error processes in the manufacturing sites." (p. i)

Thus, Toyota personnel created the system by experimenting with different ideas. To succeed using this approach, Ohno and his team had to do experiments in a systematic and scientific manner. The foundation of TPS was well-established by the mid 1950s [4].

Ohno emphasizes the practical nature of TPS:

"Thus, since the Toyota production system has been created from actual practices in the factories of Toyota, it has a strong feature of emphasizing practical effects, and actual practice and implementation over theoretical analysis." (p. i)

There is no theory in TPS as far as Mr. Ohno is concerned [4].

Explaining TPS to people – what it was, how it worked, and how to implement it – was very difficult. Ohno said:

"...even in Japan it was difficult for the people of outside companies to understand our system; still less was it possible for the foreign people to understand it." (p. i)

Many books and articles written in Japanese in the late 1970s and early 1980s describe various aspects of Toyota's production system. But a complete description of the system was not available to the Japanese public. So TPS remained difficult for people to understand.

Professor Yasuhiro Monden was the first to provide a comprehensive description of Toyota's production system to an English-speaking audience. He wrote an excellent book, published in 1983, titled: *Toyota Production System: Practical Approach to Production Management* [3]. Mr. Ohno has this to say in the Foreword of Monden's book:

> "...we are very interested in how Professor Monden has 'theorized' our practice from his academic standpoint and how he has explained it to the foreign people. At the same time, we wish to read and study this book for our own future progress." (p. i)

This is a nice bit of humility on Ohno's part; the student (Monden) learns from the teacher (Ohno) and the teacher learns from the student.

So what was Professor Monden trying to do? He was trying to address another practical problem; to help English-speaking business people understand and implement Toyota's production system so that they too could improve productivity and reduce costs. Monden said:

> "...the author's chief purpose of publishing this book is to offer some support to the companies in the U.S. and elsewhere that are making efforts to improve produc-

tivity, thereby promoting friendship between Japan and many countries." (p. v)

More specifically,

"...the central mission of this book is to develop a 'theory' to the 'practices' of Toyota manufacturing methods." (p. vi)

Professor Monden correctly thought this could best be accomplished by explaining the methods systematically and within a theoretical framework. Monden describes theory as follows:

"It is a process of building an ideal model of the real, empirical objects using the following procedures:

• Abstracting from the empirical [real] world the important factors which seem most relevant to the research objective.
• Connecting the selected factors in a logical way.

Our research objective is to build a practically applicable model; that is, this model must be able to be utilized for each company to prepare and implement the actual system of production management... the structure of goals-means relationships...[is] described as a 'theory' in this book." (p. vi-vii)

Professor Monden is saying that the framework he created to interpret and represent Toyota's production system is theory, not the Toyota production system itself which is real. Further, note that Professor Monden is using a theoretical construct for a practical purpose: to help people understand and implement Toyota's production system.

Most people have not read Professor Monden's 1983 book, so they probably did not come to view Lean incorrectly as theory from him (Note: you should become familiar with his excellent work [5]). Maybe they read it in the 1996 book *Lean Thinking*, by Womack and Jones [6]. No, that book did not use the word "theory" even one time. So how did so many people come to view Lean as a theory?

Some people have adopted the phrase "Lean theory" in reference to Lean principles or foundational concepts of Lean management such as the elimination of waste [7]. Others characterize Lean as a philosophy to call attention to the "basic way of thinking," but then extend this representation of Lean into the realm of theory. Still others refer to Lean as a theory in the context of ideas which must be then converted into practice. And maybe some people are just trying to create an impression of being knowledgeable or scholarly.

What has happened is that people innocently, but incorrectly, insert a meaning or perspective that was never spoken of or intended by the originators of Lean management – all of whom where practically-oriented working people. This, coupled with using the wrong definition of theory or mixing up theory and practice, has led to ambiguity and confusion that is not helpful.

It is odd that when a real company accomplishes something in the real world, and does so consistently over decades, some people call it "theory." It doesn't make any sense to do so; the thinking is illogical, unless the intent is to obfuscate for the purpose of avoiding some type of loss [8]. People may refer to Lean as a theory because they have an ulterior motive or are invoking a defensive mechanism to resist change. Perhaps they want to discredit Lean management or cast doubt on its effectiveness, and thus maintain the status quo. Others may be so detached from value creating activities, such as finance, information technology, engineering, or sales, that anything different from what they currently know appears theoretical to them.

I imagine that if Mr. Ohno were alive today, he'd be very annoyed to know that Toyota's management system, also known as Lean management, is thought by many people to be theory. In his foreword to Monden's book twenty-five years ago, Ohno said:

> "No longer is [productivity] solely an economic problem; now it presents a serious political problem in the form of trade frictions. At such a time it would be our great pleasure if the Toyota production system we invented could be of service to the problem of America productivity... Therefore, we hope and expect that another effective American production system will be created utilizing this book for reference." (p. i-ii)

In other words, Toyota was facing a practical political problem in the form of trade friction with the United States government, and one way of handling this was to share Toyota's practical approach to production management.

Shame on us if we fall into the trap of thinking Lean is theory. It can only hurt us as individuals, as well as the global competitiveness of U.S. manufacturing and service businesses.

Notes

[1] *The American Heritage College Dictionary*, third edition, Houghton Mifflin Company, New York, NY, 1997, p. 1406

[2] Toyota production system (TPS) is the name given to Toyota's system of manufacturing. It is a sub-set of their overall management system called "The Toyota Way." Companies that seek to emulate Toyota's management system are said to be practicing "Lean management," and can do so in ways that are either high- or low-fidelity representations. In most cases Lean management, as it has been understood and practiced thus far, is low-fidelity versions of TPS or TMS.

[3] T. Ohno in *Toyota Production System: Practical Approach to Production Management*, Industrial Engineering and Management Press, Y. Monden, Norcross, GA, 1983

[4] T. Ohno, *Toyota Production System*, Productivity Press, Portland, OR, 1988. Ohno did not use the word "theory" in his book.

[5] Y. Monden, *Toyota Production System: An Integrated Approach to Just-In-Time*, third edition, Industrial Engineering and Management Press, Norcross, GA, 1998. Prof. Monden has written several other fine books including: *Toyota Management System: Linking the Seven Key Functional Areas*, Productivity Press, Portland, OR, 1993. See http://www.productivitypress.com

[6] D. Womack and D. Jones, *Lean Thinking*, Simon & Schuster, New York, NY, 1996

[7] The eight wastes are: defects, transportation, overproduction, waiting, processing, movement, inventory, and behaviors. The eighth waste, behaviors, was identified and characterized in "Lean Behaviors," M.L. Emiliani, *Management Decision*, Vol. 36, No. 9, pp. 615-631, 1998

[8] An earlier system of management, Scientific Management (c. 1882-1950) was likewise never presented by its creators, who were practical workers and managers, as theory. See F.W. Taylor, *The Principles of Scientific Management*, Harper & Brothers Publishers, New York, NY, 1911. Taylor uses the word "theory" three times in his book and "theories" once, all in the context of challenging conventional views. Scientific Management had always been presented as a practical way to improve the work and cooperation between the management and the workers. Opponents of scientific management viewed it as impractical and problematic in various ways, and claimed Scientific Management was an "abstract theory" to discredit it. The fiercest critics of Scientific Management were organized labor unions, whose leaders apparently sensed a devastating loss

of membership should large numbers of companies implement Scientific Management. They tried to prevent or eliminate the Scientific Management system in companies that did business with the U.S. government through legislative intervention. The main criticisms presented by organized labor were easily refuted when Scientific Management was properly applied. See C. B. Thompson, *Scientific Management: A Collection of the More Significant Articles Describing The Taylor System of Management*, Harvard University Press, Cambridge, MA, 1914, pp. 26-48 and 610-635; H.B. Drury, *Scientific Management: A History and Criticism*, third edition, Studies in History, Economics and Public Law, the Faculty of Political Science of Columbia University, Columbia University Press, 1922, republished by AMS Press, Inc., New York, NY, 1968, p. 39 and pp. 210-263; Harlow S. Person in *Scientific Management in American Industry*, Harlow S. Person, editor, The Taylor Society, Harper and Brothers Publishers, New York, NY, 1929, chapter 1, pp. 18-21; and "Testimony Before the Special House Committee" in *Scientific Management: Comprising Shop Management, Principles of Scientific Management, Testimony Before the House Committee*, F.W. Taylor, with foreword by Harlow S. Person, Harper & Brothers Publishers, New York, NY, 1947.

Quotations from *Toyota Production System: Practical Approach to Production Management* are reprinted with permission of Yasuhiro Monden.

8 Know Your Competition

*Lean management advocates have a lot of convincing facts
and figures on their side to support the view that more companies should adopt Lean. Despite this, Lean remains a very
tough sell to most executives. This begs the question; do
Lean advocates truly understand what they are up against
with regards to competing methods of wealth creation?
There are a lot of easier ways to create wealth than Lean
management, even though most end up creating a big mess.*

Advocates of Lean management are a passionate group of
people who really want to help managers understand business
from new perspectives that will yield better results. Their
heart is surely in the right place, but do they fully understand
or acknowledge what they are up against? Are their strategies
and tactics good enough to convince more than a few executives here or there that Lean is a better management system?

Let's start by examining how large numbers of people are
trained to become senior managers. In the following para-
graphs I will present a general scenario, not a universal scenario. I simplify certain details for the purpose of establishing
a clearer view of the challenge that Lean advocates face. A
central feature is the classification of management systems
and managers into two types: zero-sum and non-zero-sum.

Zero-sum is the common mode of thinking and action found
in conventional management practice. Simply put, winners
gain at the expense of losers. Obviously, not all executives
who subscribe to conventional zero-sum management exe-

cute one hundred percent of their duties in a zero-sum fashion. Nevertheless, zero-sum executives are usually wealth destroyers, even though it may not look like that. In contrast, Lean, REAL Lean [1], is a non-zero-sum management system intended to benefit all key stakeholders.

The common route for becoming a senior manager is to first obtain an undergraduate degree from an accredited university. Future managers gain admission to the university and declare a major in one of the schools, typically business, engineering, or arts & sciences. They go about taking their courses. Professors do a lot of talking on different topics, but what is far more interesting is what they don't say.

Future managers were probably never advised explicitly by professors of the risks of zero-sum thinking or the benefits of non-zero-sum thinking in the real world, the workplace. If one or two professors out of the forty or more professors they had as an undergraduate did tell them that zero-sum thinking was a bad way to do business, then that probably didn't count for much. If it was so important, every professor would have said something. But they didn't.

Neither the university nor the school they attended fifteen, twenty, or thirty years ago had a policy that warned of the risks of zero-sum thinking in business. And there was no expression of non-zero-sum business principles that students had to learn as the fundamental basis of their undergraduate curriculum [2,3].

They didn't hear anything from the top university administrators about the risks of zero-sum thinking. When graduation came, the distinguished commencement speaker didn't mention it either.

How important can this be if over the course of four years only one or two professors talked about the real-world problems that zero-sum thinking generates? Those must have been the wing-nut professors.

So they graduate from college and get a job. They enter the workforce and, of course, immediately gain a boss. The first boss can be very influential to a new college graduate. The boss' view of business can easily shape a new employee's view of the company and of business. Who will they get? A zero-sum or non-zero-sum type of boss?

My own informal surveys indicate that one or two out of the ten or so bosses a person has over their first fifteen years at work will be the non-zero-sum type of boss. The rest are zero-sum bosses. So it is more likely that a new employee's first boss will be a zero-sum thinker. If instead they not get a non-zero-sum boss, it won't be long before they do get a zero-sum boss. And then another, and another…

Let's say the first boss is a zero-sum boss. What is the new employee likely to think as he or she witnesses the boss work through their zero-sum bag of tricks and creates wasteful conflicts? They might think it is not right to do those kinds of things. The new employee may also think back to their college education and say to themselves:

"I never heard a professor say 'Business is defined as a zero-sum activity. The only way to win is at other peo-

ple's expense'. But I also never heard a professor say
'Non-zero-sum thinking is a better way to do business'."

So the new employee might think zero-sum is the company-
approved way of doing business. The boss is the boss because
he or she must be good at their job, and management apparently promotes people who do things as my boss does.
Therefore, I should learn how my boss does things.

New employees will also learn how to do things from non-
zero-sum bosses. But if eighty percent or more of bosses are
the zero-sum type, then the odds are against being able to put
to use much of what the non-zero-sum boss taught you.
Despite this, it turns out that non-zero-sum bosses make
strong favorable impressions on subordinates. They typically
revere this type of boss and remember them dearly. But it is
not because these bosses were easy; it was because they
exhibited many value-added behaviors such as fairness, trust,
patience, consistency, could admit a mistake, supported their
people, etc. They learned a lot and they contributed a lot with
this type of boss. It's nice to have some good memories.

But people tend to not replicate the non-zero-sum boss.
Instead, they replicate the zero-sum bosses because that is the
way the herd thinks and acts. If you want to be part of the in-
group and advance within the company, it is best not to go
against the herd. Doing so will get you a one-way ticket to the
out-group.

After five or ten years in the workplace, promising managers
will often obtain an MBA degree. Once again, professors will
not have spoken explicitly of the risks of zero-sum thinking

or the benefits of non-zero-sum thinking. Actually, the organizational behavior professor did talk about dangers of zero-sum thinking, but everybody knows that while organizational behavior is a very interesting course, it is kind-of irrelevant. Besides, the human resources department is not a power center in most organizations; top managers don't listen much to human resources. Once again neither the university nor the business school had a policy that warned students of the risks of zero-sum thinking, and there was no statement of non-zero-sum business principles that students had to learn as the fundamental basis of their MBA curriculum.

As people rise up through the ranks, it is not long before their responsibilities become very closely tied to one thing that is of great interest to the president or chief executive officer: wealth creation. It is an important function of the executive, and the expectation must be fulfilled. The question is how do you do it?

As one's duties begin to more clearly become part of the company's wealth-creating activities, managers will begin to participate in wealth creation using the methods that they learned in the years since graduating from college. They are familiar methods, and managers will have lots of practical experience which proved to them time and time again that the methods work. Besides managers who are near the top of the corporate hierarchy must, by definition, have done a good job. Thus, there is absolutely no indication of any need for re-training.

So here is the problem: the Lean management advocates want to get executives to see a better way of doing business. The fact that it contradicts nearly everything they have learned the last twenty or thirty years should not be a barrier. But it is.

So what specifically must Lean management advocates confront? They are competing against other wealth creation methods. There are three main routes to wealth creation in business:

1) Conventional management. Key characteristics are that it is a defensive posture, sellers' market, company-first, zero-sum (asymmetrical) system of management.
2) Lean management. Done correctly, it is an offensive posture, buyers' market, customer-first, non-zero-sum (symmetrical) system of management.
3) Hybrid batch-and-queue / Lean. A undesirable middle ground that that is common today [4].

That any president or CEO of a company which operates in competitive markets would willingly choose or stick to the first route is amazing, since they'll probably tell you their company exists in a market-based economy. That means they recognize customers have choices and they are responsive to their customers. Yet there is a glaring inconsistency in what is said compared to what is actually done. In any event, ninety-eight percent or more of companies are conventionally managed or managed in a hybrid fashion.

The path to wealth creation for most organizations, surprisingly, is not through customer satisfaction [5]. That is simply a hoped-for outcome of management's narrowly focused wealth creation efforts. However, this will be impossible to realize with a zero-sum system of management, where even customer's interests are fair game in management's efforts to create corporate wealth. In other words, it is acceptable to marginalize cash-paying customer's interests as long as it creates corporate wealth. Huh?

Conventional management relies on the "CEO playbook" to execute its zero-sum wealth creation game plan. Some of the primary plays in the game plan include legislative and regulatory means to assist in management's efforts to create wealth such as easing the application of anti-trust laws, limiting labor union eligibility, restricting overtime pay, reducing disclosure requirements, changing accounting rules, extend patent duration, seek trade restrictions, limit minimum wages, etc.

Management can do many other things without the help of elected or appointed government officials to create wealth. These include laying people off (elective), closing facilities, share-buy-back, acquire, merge, or divest assets change accounting methods, squeeze suppliers, outsource or off-shore work, cut pay and benefits, reduce quality or durability, etc. Senior managers are particularly fond of these plays because they yield quick hits to the bottom line and pump up the stock price.

In both cases, the list of things that can be done to create wealth, from a cost cutting perspective, is much longer than this. There are, of course, additional plays in the wealth creation playbook such as new product or service development that, while very important, are not the focus of this discussion.

What the CEO has in front of them is a simple *á la carte* menu of zero-sum items that they can pick from at any time and use over and over again if necessary, to transfer wealth from someone else to the company. It is a closed system – that is, the pie can not get any larger – of zero-sum wealth transfer. These are things managers learn about in school, or they see other respected business leaders doing these things. Their use is validated and accepted in the real world, and it even brings fame and glory for being a "tough manager" who is able to make "hard decisions."

It should also be mentioned that the conventional, zero-sum management system is a safe-haven for psychopathic supervisors, managers, and executives. The management system fits perfectly with their selfish personality characteristics. However, this comes at a cost. Psychopathic managers inflict great harm on employees (for example, expensive stress-related illnesses), suppliers (for example, squeezing them on price and foolishly not expecting them to retaliate in the future), customers (for example, giving them poor quality and foolishly not expecting them to shop elsewhere), etc. Lean people would see this type of manager as having behavior patterns that are inconsistent with the "Respect for People" principle. A company will not survive long-term with systemic psychopathic management.

Creating wealth from waste is not taught in college and is not well understood by top managers. It is a non-zero-sum open system of wealth creation where the pie gets bigger. So instead of simply re-distributing existing wealth contained within the slices of a fixed-size pie, which anyone can do, managers grow the pie so that the owner of each slice realizes greater wealth. Simply put, senior managers and influential investors will not favor wealth creation methods they do not understand or perceive to be slow at increasing wealth.

This is what Lean management must compete against. It is much more challenging for managers to be on the offensive, versus taking a defensive posture in the marketplace. It is much more challenging to respond to a buyers' market with a "customer-first" attitude. And it is much more challenging to operate a non-zero-sum system of management designed to produce more balanced and symmetrical outcomes among the key stakeholders.

The truth is that senior managers don't need Lean management to do the kinds of things that boards of directors and shareholders expect them to do, which is to increase sales, gross profit, cash flow, inventory turns, working capital turnover, etc. Many other things can be done which are much easier and faster to implement, none of which require specialized re-training in order to see waste, unevenness, and unreasonableness. And besides, non-zero-sum management is not seen as business-like.

It is likely that Lean management will never win the competition among wealth creation methods. After nearly thirty years of effort, perhaps two percent of companies of any size have adopted REAL Lean management. At that rate, it will be three hundred years before twenty percent of companies practice Lean management. Alternatively, two percent or so could be the steady-state figure because most companies revert back to conventional management when there is a change in leadership or a change in ownership [6].

Lean is a niche management system; one in a long line of management systems designed to improve processes. In recent times, this includes the six sigma tool and Total

Quality Management (TQM). Is it any wonder why Lean, six sigma, and TQM are often incorrectly seen as the same thing and eventually relegated to flavor-of-the-month status? It's because the CEO playbook consistently wins the competition [6] despite the fact that the plays in the playbook are messy to execute and create loads of conflict, generate enemies with long memories, lead to opportunism among key stakeholders, and makes a company more vulnerable to major errors that could threaten its existence.

Indeed, an earlier system of management called Scientific Management [7,8] also competed against these methods for seventy years – and lost [9]. It has been a one hundred twenty five year struggle for process improvement advocates to convince conventionally-minded managers to do something different that will better serve all stakeholders. What has fundamentally changed that would help improve this situation? Perhaps it is all the new knowledge that has emerged in recent years about how to correctly practice Lean management.

One would think that many more companies would adopt Lean if executives were better informed about how to correctly practice Lean management. However, this may not have as much of a positive effect as one might imagine, and it could even have a negative effect. The emergence of more books and training programs on how to correctly implement Lean management could highlight just how far the company and its managers have to go and also create confusion.

The new knowledge that has emerged in recent years is typically specialized in that it discusses the application of Lean management in the different functional areas of a business.

This could intimidate executives because it appears to them to be an overwhelming challenge that is not realistic or therefore not worth pursuing. This has already become a common reaction among executives [10]. So despite the good efforts of Lean advocates, the Lean journey may not look like an attractive opportunity to presidents or CEOs steeped in conventional management practice and who already know the simple zero-sum playbook very well.

Finally, let's not forget that top managers who practice Lean well will be less visible, receive fewer rewards, are required to separate themselves from their peer group, must mentally switch from defensive ways of doing business to offensive, and also challenge their long-held views of corporate purpose, in addition to their views of economics, politics, and society. What's the incentive to question everything? What's the incentive to make these big changes?

Lean advocates have a lot more work to do to know the competition that they are up against. Once they do that they can identify practical countermeasures, and perhaps convince twenty percent of companies of the merits of Lean management in only fifty years.

In the end, large numbers of executives will not adopt Lean management until they view it as a superior approach to wealth creation compared to the CEO playbook.

Notes

[1] Where REAL Lean embodies the two key principles, "Continuous Improvement" and "Respect for People." Fake Lean exists when only the "Continuous Improvement" principle is practiced.

[2] As a result of the numerous financial scandals that occurred between 1995 and 2005, AACSB International, the accrediting body for business schools, has created a document that encourages business school educators to strengthen ethics education. See "Ethics Education in Business Schools," 2004, http://www.aacsb.edu/resource_centers/ethicsedu/EETF-report-6-25-04.pdf.

[3] For an excellent expression of non-zero-sum business principles, see the Caux Round Table *Principles for Business* (1994), http://www.cauxround-table.org/documents/Principles%20for%20Business.PDF

[4] Hybrid conventional / Lean management does not function well and should be avoided because zero-sum actions eclipse non-zero-sum actions. It also causes a great deal of confusion among stakeholders.

[5] The proof of that is the few businesses that excel at satisfying customers, many of which serve luxury goods or services markets. See "Customer Service Champs," J. McGregor, *BusinessWeek*, 5 March 2007, pp. 52-64

[6] See for example, *Better Thinking, Better Results: Case Study and Analysis of an Enterprise-Wide Lean Transformation*, B. Emiliani, with D. Stec, L. Grasso, and J. Stodder, second edition, The CLBM, LLC, Wethersfield, Conn., 2007, for a real world example of how conventional management can win over Lean management.

[7] In a nutshell, Scientific Management can be described as a system of production management that, if done correctly, resulted in a much more efficient batch-and-queue (push) production system; 2-3 times more efficient than basic batch-and-queue production. Its application was later extended to non-production activities and to non-manufacturing industries. Its main foci were "betterment" of the work and "cooperation." Some of its principles, methods, and tools are the same or similar to that found in Lean management. See F.W. Taylor, *The Principles of Scientific Management*, Harper & Brothers Publishers, New York, NY, 1911; *Scientific Management in American Industry*, Harlow S. Person, editor, The Taylor Society, Harper and Brothers Publishers, New York, NY, 1929; and *Scientific Management: Comprising Shop Management, Principles of Scientific Management, Testimony Before the House Committee*, F.W. Taylor, with foreword by Harlow S. Person, Harper & Brothers Publishers, New York, NY, 1947.

[8] Scientific Management was an early attempt to create a non-zero-sum management system. It was seen as a better way to create wealth. See H.B. Drury, *Scientific Management: A History and Criticism*, third edition, Studies in History, Economics and Public Law, the Faculty of Political Science of Columbia University, Columbia University Press, 1922, republished by AMS Press, Inc., New York, NY, 1968, p. 254 and S. Chase, *The Tragedy of Waste*, The Macmillan Company, New York, NY, 1925. Technically, however, it retains zero-sum features because it is still a batch-and-queue (push) system. However, Scientific Management is much less zero-sum compared to simple batch-and-queue management thinking and practice. The rationale for improved human relations and the work analysis methods developed by the leaders of Scientific Management (or separately by others) were major advances in management thinking and practice.

[9] The life span of Scientific Management was from 1882 to about 1950, after which its ideas and methods were subsumed, either in whole or part, into general management.

[10] Anything that proceeds in the direction of making things more complex for executives, whether in fact or in appearance, will likely not meet with much success.

9 "It's Overwhelming"

Executives who are properly trained in Lean management will typically view the challenge of implementing Lean as overwhelming. On the up-side, they are finally starting to see the mountains of waste, unevenness, and unreasonableness in their business processes and in their leadership. On down-side, by saying "It's overwhelming," they are usually making mental preparations to avoid implementing REAL Lean. Here are some tips on getting over the hump.

I've been training executives in Lean management for a decade. About half-way through the training most executives begin to realize the scope and challenge of REAL Lean, as a management system, the new knowledge they must acquire, the old knowledge they must let go of, and the actual practice they must engage in every day. They have a common reaction: "It's overwhelming."

Red flags immediately go up because this is an early indicator that Lean management appears to them to be too difficult and therefore possibly not worth doing. As officers of the company, executives are paid to confront change and manage risks. With REAL Lean, the change is big and the risk is small, but the risk is made to look much larger than it really is to delay taking action. In most cases, the risks incurred by not doing Lean will be much greater.

Lean is clearly a BIG opportunity. Executives who do not sense the opportunity or feel overwhelmed need to further investigate Lean, rather than back off. They make a lot of money in salary, stock options, bonuses, and other forms of compensation. But that doesn't help them rise to the challenge of REAL Lean management. Instead, they will come up with lots of different excuses such as: "Lean is a threat; I might look stupid; I don't want to disrupt the business; we don't have the talent to do this; we don't have time; It's too hard; that's not how we do things," etc.

Executives are able to wiggle out of Lean because, obviously, they have the power to do so. But there is another, more important factor; they are allowed to wiggle away. What stakeholder is saying to the CEO: "You need to do Lean"? Not customers, not employees, not suppliers, and not even investors [1]. In general, the stakeholders have rather low expectations of top managers, surprisingly investors as well, because their frame of reference is the average business performance that conventional management practice yields [2]. Also, they tend to give a lot of credit to leaders simply because of the position they hold.

We can look at this from another direction. That is, most executives misjudge the Lean challenge. This is a common occurrence caused by simple decision-making traps such as framing, anchoring, status-quo, sunk-cost, or confirming evidence [3]. They incorrectly assume Lean must be done in addition to their current workload, rather than as part of – or better yet – instead of their current workload. Misjudging things is a human foible. For example, golf looks easy to most people but it is actually very difficult. Conversely, playing guitar looks difficult to most people but is relatively easy. Mistaken impressions and incorrect assumptions motivate managers to avoid a challenge, not to engage it.

Lean management is not so difficult. It has two key principles, some counterintuitive concepts, several simple methods and tools, and mostly seventh- or eighth-grade math. But executives make it difficult when they adopt Lean half-heartedly, practice only once in a while, and don't bother to keep thinking and learning about Lean. As a result, they have difficulty grasping the many nuances and inter-connections.

Saying "It's overwhelming" can also be code for "We don't know where to start." If a subordinate said that to an executive, you know exactly what their response would be: "You're smart; go figure it out," or "Go talk to Susan." Not knowing where to start when confronted with the new Lean challenge is understandable, but it is not that difficult; you simply "Go figure it out" [4] or "Go talk to Bob."

Take a sport, a musical instrument, or some other new endeavor that you wish to gain proficiency. Where do you start? Whether you begin alone or with the help of a teacher, you will probably do the following:

- Keep it simple
- Take it one step at a time
- Focus on the fundamentals

These are not difficult things to do. What is difficult is to make a long-term commitment to them and to develop the discipline to practice every day, whether you feel like it or not.

Art Byrne, the retired president and CEO of The Wiremold Company, is a highly regarded Lean practitioner. He did these things. In addition, he was greatly influenced by three fundamental books on Lean management:

- *Toyota Production System* by Taiichi Ohno
- *The SMED System* by Shigeo Shingo
- *A Study of the Toyota Production System* by Shigeo Shingo

And he was also influenced by some excellent kaizen teachers. You can go a very long way on the journey to REAL Lean by doing what Art Byrne and his management team did [5]. You can also go even further.

Let's put this into perspective. Figure 1 illustrates a relationship between four skill levels in baseball and four types of management systems, each of which also requires a certain skill level. You can use it to estimate where you are as a manager and where your company is in relation to a familiar standard: major league baseball.

Little league ball is analogous to basic batch-and-queue management of a manufacturing or service business. College ball represents a more efficient form of batch-and-queue management akin to early 1900s Scientific Management. The minor league represents the hybrid batch-and-queue / Lean management system, also known as "Fake Lean" or "Imitation Lean." Lastly, the major leagues represent REAL Lean.

The baseball leagues and management systems are shown next to a logarithmic scale to indicate the existence of different skills levels within a particular classification.

Figure 1. Levels of sport and management achievement.

Major League	1000	REAL Lean ———— 2%
Minor League	100	Hybrid B&Q / Lean
College Ball	10	Efficient B&Q 98%
Little League	1	Basic B&Q

Today most companies are in the efficient batch-and-queue, or hybrid batch-and-queue / Lean management classification. If a management team can break into the major league, REAL Lean, then they truly begin to distinguish themselves. Over time, the executive team will be able to say that they did something that few people or companies in the world have done.

Figure 1 is important from another perspective. Executives of big companies often say or think they are world-class, but the rhetoric usually does not match the reality. They typically manage using efficient batch-and-queue or hybrid batch-and-queue / Lean management, both of which are strongly rooted in conventional zero-sum management practice. So the challenge is to raise the skill level so that the management team and the company can enter into the major league of non-zero-sum REAL Lean.

If you think REAL Lean is overwhelming, then you'll never become part of the major league. Avoiding this outcome requires at least the following: humility, willingness to learn new things through classroom training, books, and daily on-the-job practice, and enduring motivation. In other words, you've got to think and work a lot harder than you have been if you want to get into the major leagues. It will not come to you. And it can not be delegated to lower levels within the company.

Imagine what a ball player has to do to break into a major league, or what a musician must do to perform at a professional level. Executives have to do the same types of things and have similar levels of commitment. They will have to do even more than ball players or musicians because they are responsible for hundreds or thousands people and must understand and try to balance the needs of their key stakeholders. Executives will need to do simple but effective things to stay on track, such as create visual controls to serve as reminders of how they need to think and what they need to do. And they will need to support each other when one member falters, as real teams do.

I'd like you to consider the following simple two-step approach. First, set a goal to learn the Lean management system, but do not specify a time-frame for doing so. Second, start learning and practicing Lean management every day at work for eight to ten hours, for everything you think and do. Within a few short years, you'll be amazed at the Lean thinking and Lean doing skills that you will have developed. What do you do next? You keep going. Continue pursuing your goal to learn the Lean management system and continue to practice every day at work for eight to ten hours. In a few more years, you'll be even more amazed at the Lean thinking and Lean doing skills that you will have developed. What do you do next? You keep going; you just keep going.

You cannot implement the Lean management system alone. Lean is a broad-based participative approach to managing and improving an enterprise. You'll need to get everyone involved: junior executives, middle managers, supervisors, and associates. But they won't get involved unless you are leading the way. To do that, you must know what you are talking about, which only comes by studying and practicing Lean management every day.

Please don't ever fall into the trap of saying: "The reason we haven't been able to do more is because of middle-manager resistance." Middle-managers who resist Lean are simply responding to executive's implicit and explicit cues. They will resist Lean if they feel they will be blamed for errors. That's senior management's problem, not middle-manager's problem. Prove it to yourself by doing a root cause analysis of this problem. You'll see that the causes of middle-manager resistance loop back onto senior management.

Senior managers are well-paid and their job is to confront change and manage risks. Those who receive exceptional pay should do exceptional things, and not be stuck in the minor leagues doing what everyone else is doing.

Also think for a moment about what people do not expect of executives. Let's start with employees. They do not expect you to coast to retirement; make business more complicated and more difficult for them; treat them poorly (snap judgments, blame, etc.); use tricks that help the business short-term but undercut it for the long-term; create conflicts among stakeholders; build more bureaucracy; overlook threats in the marketplace; continue to repeat mistakes; be a zero-sum leader who creates waste, unevenness, and unreasonableness; and so on. You can bet suppliers, customers, and investors do not expect these things of you either.

James Mapes Dodge, former chairman of the board of The Link-Belt Company and a staunch promoter of an earlier system of management, Scientific Management, had this to say on October 13, 1911 [6]:

> "Probably with all of us it is more difficult to accept a modification of a belief than to absorb a most startling or revolutionary new idea which does not call for any reversal of a notion to which we have tenaciously held. So in this matter of management it was, and is, and always will be essential for us to keep a hopeful equilibrium during transition from our old to our new love; and this transition is certain to be a trying one.
>
> In the establishments with which I am connected, conversion came slowly to nearly all, and some of those who, it would seem, should logically have accepted the innovation with avidity, seemed temperamentally incapable of such acceptance. Those who live entirely in the present, without thought of the future or of the past, can easily acquire the habit of doing things in a new way; but those having active minds are apt to waver between the necessity of advancing a decision and the fear of error born of caution and imagination [over-thinking things].
>
> ...instead of investigating in an open-minded way the

logic and results, they elect to question every minor step and consider that they must be accorded a complete vindication and proof of the other man's ideas before they are willing to lessen their grip on preconceived and opposing convictions.

It is therefore essential, in order to use the new system of management, that a man have within him a desire to travel in that direction, and that he aid to the best of his ability in the removal of small, real or imaginary obstructions, rather than hold back and allow all his progress to be brought about [dictated by] by the pressure of the breeching [worker resistance], or the pull at the halter [manager resistance].

...under no circumstances should anything be done which has even the appearance of taking advantage of him [the workmen]. He must appreciate that his interests and those of his employer are mutual, and that their happiness and success depend upon mutual trust and consideration. If employers think that by the introduction of Scientific Management they can gain an advantage over the workers, they are making a serious mistake and wasting their efforts in what will eventually turn out to their great and lasting disadvantage.

...[nineteenth century English philosopher] Herbert Spencer [7] said that there is a principle which is proof against all argument, and which cannot fail to keep a man in everlasting ignorance; this principle is to condemn before investigating."

These same words apply today to senior managers who wish to transition from old-time zero-sum conventional management to new non-zero-sum REAL Lean management.

So off you go. First, set a goal to learn the Lean management system, but do not set a time-frame for doing so. Second, start learning and practicing Lean management every day for eight to ten hours for everything you think and do [4]. And keep going.

Along the way, please be sure to put a plan in place for when the inevitable happens: a change in leadership or a change in company ownership. You don't want your Lean efforts to be extinguished by a different management team.

Notes

[1] Occasionally you will find a customer, employee, supplier, or investor that will suggest to senior managers that they adopt Lean management. But this not a widespread phenomenon, largely due to the many misunderstanding that people possess about Lean management.

[2] Operating the conventional management system at above average levels is typically achieved by zero-sum financial engineering, which, of course, can be ethical and legal, or unethical and illegal. Executives should understand and respond to the explicit and implicit expectations of employees, suppliers, customer and investors. They will find many areas of similarity and some differences. Lean is a management system that is better able to respond to the mostly shared interests and expectations among stakeholders, and yields better financial and non-financial results.

[3] All executives should be well-versed in the common decision-making traps. See "The Hidden Traps in Decision Making," J. Hammond, R. Keeney, and H. Raiffa, *Harvard Business Review*, September-October 1998, Vol. 76, No. 5, pp. 47-58

[4] There are some excellent books that can help develop your Lean thinking skills and guide your Lean transformation including: T. Ohno, *Toyota Production System*, Productivity Press, Portland, OR, 1988; Y. Monden, *Toyota Management System: Linking the Seven Key Functional Areas*, Productivity Press, Portland, OR, 1993; M. Cowley and E. Domb, *Beyond Strategic Planning: Effective Corporate Action with Hoshin Planning*, Butterworth-Heinemann, New York, NY, 1997; Y. Monden, *Toyota Production System: An Integrated Approach to Just-In-Time*, third edition, Industrial Engineering and Management Press, Norcross, GA, 1998; S. Basu, *Corporate Purpose: Why it Matters More than Strategy*, Garland Publishing, New York, NY, 1999; B. Maskell and B. Baggaley, *Practical Lean Accounting*, Productivity Press, New York, NY, 2003; T. Fujimoto, *The Evolution of a Manufacturing System at Toyota*, Oxford University Press, New York, NY, 1999; J. Liker, *The Toyota Way*, McGraw-Hill, New York, NY, 2004; S. Hino, *Inside the Mind of Toyota*, Productivity Press, New York, NY, 2006; *Better Thinking, Better Results: Case Study and Analysis of an Enterprise-Wide Lean Transformation*, B. Emiliani, with D. Stec, L. Grasso, and J. Stodder, second edition, The CLBM, LLC, Wethersfield, Conn., 2007

[5] See *Better Thinking, Better Results: Case Study and Analysis of an Enterprise-Wide Lean Transformation*, B. Emiliani, with D. Stec, L. Grasso, and J. Stodder, second edition, The CLBM, LLC, Wethersfield, Conn., 2007

[6] "The Spirit in Which Scientific Management Should be Approached," J.M. Dodge in *Scientific Management: First Conference at the Amos Tuck School Dartmouth College*, The Plimpton Press, Norwood, Mass, 1912, pp. 145-146 and 151-152

[7] For more information on Herbert Spencer, see http://en.wikipedia.org/wiki/Herbert_Spencer

10 Neglected Opportunities

Thirty years into the development and application of Scientific Management, the proponents of the system began to realize their implementation errors and neglected opportunities. Thirty years into application of Lean management, the proponents of the system have begun to realize their implementation errors and neglected opportunities. The similarities between the two are stunning, despite a separation of over eighty years. It is a stark reminder of our collective failure to learn important practical lessons from the past.

Efforts have emerged in the past few years to correct deficiencies in Lean management thinking and practice. This is a necessary and favorable development. However, much of the pain, cost, and arduous re-work we are now experiencing could have been avoided if we had interest in the successes and failures of the trailblazers who preceded us a century ago in their development and practice of a new management system.

Henry H. Farquhar, assistant professor of industrial management at Harvard Graduate School of Business Administration, presented a paper to the members of the Taylor Society in New York City on January 24, 1924 [1]. In the paper, Farquhar gave a critical analysis of Scientific Management in which he noted its many positive contributions. However, what really stands out are his keen observations on implementation errors and neglected opportunities in the advocacy and practice of the Scientific Management system.

Remarkably, every item mentioned parallels implementation

errors and neglected opportunities in the practice of the Lean management system from the late 1970s through today (external to Toyota).

<u>Then and Now</u> - The struggle to correctly measure and report costs.

> "…in the last few years much attention has been given to the establishment of 'standard costs' or standard rates for overhead distribution. If fact, I question whether the pendulum has not swung too far in this direction in that the actual cost is too often disregarded by simply taking the difference between actual and standard directly to Profit and Loss. I feel that Mr. Taylor himself would have heartily approved of setting up a normal or standard overhead rate, but that he would have most emphatically condemned our using the resulting theoretical cost figures alone without being able to compare them with the facts – the actual cost of the product, including all expenses of turning that product out." (p. 141)

Today, there is a vibrant Lean accounting movement [2] that "seeks to move from traditional cost accounting to a system that measures and motivates good business practices in the lean enterprise" [3]. Importantly, "real numbers" [4] are emphasized rather than contrived numbers that make it more difficult for financial and operating personnel to monitor and assess performance, and determine where to focus improvement efforts.

<u>Then and Now</u> – Indiscriminate application of tools to improve efficiency.

"Our most serious failure is neglecting sufficiently to analyze the particular sales, production and financial problems of the particular business before attempting to apply methods for more effective management. The fact that practically all groups particularly interested in industrial management have done likewise does not by any means excuse us who have the reputation for possessing a scientific, analytical method of attack." (p. 147)

Nearly every Lean implementation to-date has had an obsessive focus on tools, and internal and external consultants have usually applied the tools indiscriminately in order to show quick results – often in workflows that have little impact on customer satisfaction and overall business performance.

Then and Now – Excessive focus on the shop.

"…[we must extend] the same principles to the control of the total activities of the business …it is true that we have as yet barely scratched the surface in the application of the scientific method to industry, particularly as regards departments other than the shop…" (p. 143, 144)

Likewise, nearly every Lean implementation over the last thirty years has focused on improving operations, with little or no application to other parts of the business.

Then and Now – Difficulty standardizing work and leaving standardization to the workers.

"…it is the management's duty to bring about thorough standardization and accurate planning and control

before asking the workman... to exert himself toward
increased production." (p. 144)

Senior managers generally do not recognize their responsibility to understand, create, and enforce standardized work.
They delegate it to others, which explains why most Lean
transformations suffer backslide.

<u>Then and Now</u> – Confusing terminology and failed message.

"...many managers still shy at the word 'science'...
Much of the disregard of what I believe to be fundamentally sound principles of industrial relationship...
[has been due] to a reaction of skepticism connected in
the linking of the terms 'scientific' and 'management.'

...why have our mechanisms and methods received so
much attention at the expense of the basic principles?
Why have we failed to make management and men
realize the mutuality of interest existing between
employer and employee... Is this condition due partly
to complacency, or to a lack of aggressiveness or persuasive powers on our part?

I wonder how much of our failure to impress the manager and secure the progress we desire is because we
have given more thought to training the workman than
we have to training the management?

Undoubtedly, also, our message has not been more
fully absorbed because... the easy way is usually more
attractive to the average manager. Shortcuts are partic-

ularly tempting. It is due to the fact that we have been talking calculus much of the time when the manager is still struggling with elementary algebra.

...I am afraid that we have too often given the impression to the manager that nothing which he has or does is worth much, that we have asked him as well as his workmen to 'lose face' by expecting that he 'back up' on matters, which he cannot do without losing status, as well as by failing to give credit for good work and good suggestions where credit is due." (p. 144, 149-150)

Management and worker skepticism of Lean has been with us since the late-1970s, then narrowly characterized as "Just-In-Time". In cases where skepticism has diminished or where Lean has been embraced, it is the tools that have received all of the attention, not the principles: "Continuous Improvement" and "Respect for People" [5]. The "calculus" that Lean management speaks to is non-zero-sum management practice, while the "elementary algebra" that senior managers struggle with is zero-sum management practice. Of course, it is true that we tend to treat managers that do not "get it" rather harshly, and we fail to give credit where credit is due.

Then and Now – Obsessive focus on science and not on the art.

"...while there may be a considerable management science, there is without question much in management that must remain an *art*. There must still be required the skilful exercise of human faculty, since there can be no science, for instance, of cooperation – cooperation rests not on scientific but on ethical principles... because we have not sufficiently recognized these distinctions in practice, we have fallen into a number of serious errors.

I wonder if we have sufficiently realized that, in order to live up to Mr. Taylor's ideals, the need of real leadership is even more necessary than under the older types of management...

I believe 'Scientific Management' at its best is pretty close to being the golden rule made operative in industry through the scientific method." (p. 136, 145)

In current times the "management science" is what we now call "continuous improvement," the methods, while the art of cooperation is what we now call "respect for people" [6]. The "real leadership" that Farquhar refers to is the capability for non-zero-sum thinking and practice, which of course is congruent with the "Respect for People" principle in Lean management. Indeed, this is exactly what we need today.

Then and Now – Excessive focus on money.

"Have we had the dollar so firmly fixed before our own eyes that we have assumed that the workman is similarly constituted, overlooking the workman's pride in workmanship, his logical desire to retain what he considers to be his own tools of livelihood... his trade secrets... and his desire to be a regular fellow in his own group?" (p. 146)

Old habits die hard; we tend to obsessively focus on costs and also "bean count" Lean, not realizing why it is inappropriate to do so [7]. Most workers are not motivated by money in the same way that senior managers typically are; "real leadership" understands the importance of having a clearly defined purpose [8].

Then and Now – The need to teach sound management in business schools.

> "We have not, I feel, utilized as we might the many educational institutions which are giving courses on management... It is our obligation to see that the part which the schools of business play in this training is based on a thorough understanding of what really constitutes sound management." (p. 152)

We continue to underutilize business schools and fail to communicate what really constitutes sound management. Informal coordinated efforts began in 2005 to introduce Lean management into engineering and business school curricula [9].

Then and Now – Neglecting organized labor.

> "Our relation with organized labor... must be fostered. I believe one of our great duties is to minimize those seemingly irreconcilable points of differences which may remain, and to cooperate in the solution of common problems." (p. 146-147, 152)

Labor has a lot to gain from executives who correctly understand and practice Lean management. Labor leaders themselves need to gain an accurate understanding of Lean management and, as a key stakeholder, pressure top executives to practice REAL Lean management. Customers and investors should do the same.

Then and Now – The low efficiency of management.

> "Finally, as regards our responsibilities as managers, I wish to quote the manager of one large establishment... In reply to my question as to the probable future trend of developments in his plant, he writes:
>
>> 'The most important development in our management methods In the near future will probably be improvement in management itself. We have an idea that, in general, the efficiency of management is less as the present time than the efficiency of labor.'" (p. 153)

One countermeasure for this recurring problem would be to apply standardized work for executive leadership [10].

Then and Now – The need for cooperation.

It is wise to keep in mind the practical words of Harlow S. Person [11]:

> "...management will win the cooperation of all the personnel of the enterprise, not as a matter of humanitarianism but as a matter of technical necessity. Without such cooperation all other provisions for excellence of management are impaired."

In the context of Lean management, the "Respect for People" principle is not a matter of humanitarianism but a matter of survival. Unfortunately, this fact has long been unrecognized or ignored by most executives.

Notes

[1] Henry H. Farquhar, "A Critical Analysis of Scientific Management," *Bulletin of the Taylor Society*, Vol. 9, No. 1, February 1924, in *Classics in Scientific Management: A Book of Readings*, D. Del Mar and R. Collons, The University of Alabama Press, University, Alabama, 1976, pp. 134-153

[2] For more information on Lean accounting, see http://www.leanaccountingsummit.com and http://www.leanaccountingsummit.com/LeanAccountingDefined-Target.pdf

[3] Source: http://www.igetleanaccounting.com/doyougetit.asp.

[4] See *Real Numbers: Management Accounting in a Lean Organization*, J. Cunningham and O. Fiume, Managing Times Press, Durham, NC, 2003 and *Practical Lean Accounting*, B. Maskell and B. Baggaley, Productivity Press, New York, NY, 2004

[5] "The Toyota Way 2001," Toyota Motor Corporation, internal document, Toyota City, Japan, April 2001

[6] Scientific Management was an early attempt to create a non-zero-sum management system. Its principal foci were "betterment" of the work and "cooperation." This is how today's Lean management principles, "Continuous Improvement" and "Respect for People," were conceptualized and practiced in the early 1900s. Scientific Management applied correctly, resulted in a much more efficient batch-and-queue (push) production system; 2-3 times more efficient than basic batch-and-queue production. Technically, however, it retains zero-sum features because it is still a batch-and-queue (push) system. However, Scientific Management is much less zero-sum compared to simple batch-and-queue management thinking and practice. The rationale for improved human relations and the work analysis methods developed by the leaders of Scientific Management (or separately by others) were major advances in management thinking and practice. Some of its principles, methods, and tools are the same or similar to that found in Lean management. To better understand Scientific Management, see F.W. Taylor, *The Principles of Scientific Management*, Harper & Brothers Publishers, New York, NY, 1911 and "Taylor's Testimony Before the Special House Committee" in *Scientific Management: Comprising Shop Management, Principles of Scientific Management, Testimony Before the House Committee*, F.W. Taylor, with foreword by Harlow S. Person, Harper & Brothers Publishers, New York, NY, 1947.

[7] It is inappropriate because "bean counting" Lean is a self-centered decision that is made without consideration of end-use customers, and it exposes senior management's disdain for learning and improvement.

[8] See S. Basu, *Corporate Purpose: Why it Matters More than Strategy*, Garland Publishing, New York, NY, 1999 and See http://www.toyota.co.jp/en/vision/message/index.html, as well as http://www.toyota.co.jp/en/vision/philosophy/index.html and

http://www.toyota.co.jp/en/vision/sustainability/index.html

[9] See http://www.teachinglean.org

[10] M.L. Emiliani, "Standardized Work for Executive Leadership," *Leadership and Organizational Development Journal*, Vol. 29, No. 1, pp. 24-46, 2008

[11] H.S. Person, "Shaping Your Management to Meet Developing Industrial Conditions," *Bulletin of the Taylor Society*, Vol. 7., No., 6, December 1922, re-published in *Scientific Management Since Taylor: A Collection of Authoritative Papers*, E.E. Hunt, editor, McGraw-Hill, 1924, reissued in 1972 by Hive Publishing Co., Easton, PA, pp. 129

11 Accountants and Their Cost Systems

The pioneers of Lean management, and Scientific Management before that, were almost always at odds with accountants and their cost systems. The strained relationship between office-based accounting managers and shop floor-based production managers has gone on for nearly one hundred years, but needs to come to an end as a prerequisite for advancing Lean management. Further, overcoming this problem directly addresses the sustainability of Lean issue that concerns so many people. So how do we do it?

The people with mechanical engineering or technical backgrounds who were instrumental in the establishment and evolution of Lean in operations have long been frustrated with accountants and cost accounting systems. Between 1885 and 1925, engineers were the principal architects of modern cost systems [1-3]. These engineer-accountants, as well as the Scientific Management and Lean management pioneers, were highly critical of the shortcuts and simplifications made by accountants – direct-indirect labor cost ratio, averaging overhead burdens, (averaged) standard costs, etc. – because they resulted in inaccurate and misleading cost information which was then used by top managers for decision-making; decisions that were virtually guaranteed to be poor or incorrect.

The engineer-accountants of Scientific Management era (1885-1950) and Lean pioneers after that wanted accurate cost information that reflected actual production processes. They simply wanted the facts, but could not get them because their views on cost information were largely ignored by career accounting and finance executives, especially post-1950. They voiced their frustrations in their writings, which clearly indicate the existence of two competing views of what are the facts and which facts should be used to guide day-to-day management decision-making:

- Facts on paper derived from calculations made in an office (accounting view)
- Facts derived from seeing for yourself on the shop or office floor, or "go see" in the language of Lean management (engineering view) [4].

This difference has led to long-running animosity between office-based accountants and shop floor-based production managers, which makes it impossible to function as a team with shared goals. Before we can improve the situation, let's first have a look at how the pioneers of Lean management viewed the problem.

In his 1903 paper "Shop Management" [5], Frederick Winslow Taylor (1856-1915), who was the father of Scientific Management [6], sought to overturn the long-held management accounting view that wages paid to laborers were a manufacturer's biggest problem:

> "What the workmen want from their employers beyond anything else is high wages, and what employers want from their workmen most of all is a low labor cost of manufacture.
>
> These two conditions are not diametrically opposed to one another as would appear at first glance. On the con-

trary, they can be made to go together in all classes of work, without exception, and in the writer's judgment the existence or absence of these two elements forms the best index to either good or bad management.

This book is written mainly with the object of advocating *high wages* and *low labor cost* as the foundation of the best management, of pointing out the general principles which render it possible to maintain these conditions even under the most trying circumstances, and of indicating the various steps which the writer thinks should be taken in changing from a poor system to a better type of management.

The condition of high wages and low labor cost is far from being accepted either by the average manager or the average workman as a practical working basis. It is safe to say that the majority of employers have a feeling of satisfaction when their workmen are receiving lower wages than those of their competitors. On the other hand very many workmen feel contented if they find themselves doing the same amount of work per day as other similar workmen do and yet are getting more pay for it. Employers and workmen alike should look upon both of these conditions with apprehension, as either of them are sure, in the long run, to lead to trouble and loss for both parties."

Taylor goes on to say:

"To summarize, then, what the aim in each establishment should be:

(a) That each workman should be given as far as possible the highest grade of work for which his ability and physique fit him.

(b) That each workman should be called upon to turn out the maximum amount of work which a first-rate man of his class can do and thrive.

(c) That each workman, when he works at the best pace of a first-class man, should be paid from 30 per cent to 100 per cent according to the nature of the work which he does, beyond the average of his class.

And this means *high wages* and a *low labor cost*. These conditions not only serve the best interests of the employer, but they tend to raise each workman to the highest level which he is fitted to attain by making him use his best faculties, forcing him to become and remain ambitious and energetic, and giving him sufficient pay to live better than in the past."

Taylor is presenting a radically different view of wages and labor cost that goes against the conventional wisdom possessed by managers and accountants. The real problems are: 1) management hired the wrong people or assigned people to tasks for which they are ill-suited, and 2) poor work methods (discussed in greater detail in *The Principles of Scientific Management* [6]).

Both of these lead to low wages and high labor costs for the company due to over-hiring. Improving the selection of workers and making sure they are well-suited to the work means fewer workers will be needed, but this will not be sustainable unless work methods are greatly improved. Having fewer workers and higher output will enable mangers to pay higher wages, which is what workers want, but without incurring high labor costs.

But alas, accounting systems have long had a very strong focus on wages and payroll [1,7], which are much easier to measure and criticize than process costs or the amount of work that people do.

Henry Laurence Gantt (1861-1919), a close colleague of Frederick Taylor, was a mechanical engineer, the creator of the famous Gantt chart used in project management, and noted Scientific Management practitioner and prominent management consultant [8]. He had this to say about accountants and their cost systems in a lecture given to students at Yale University in 1915 [9]:

> "Too often the system of cost accounting has been to a large extent to blame, for the systems in general use often fail to disclose the real troubles, and content themselves with blaming the shop with inefficiency.
>
> It is true that many shops are managed inefficiently, but it is also true that this inefficiency is often due to financial or selling policies over which the [factory] superintendent has no control. As a matter of fact the call for efficiency which has been so loudly proclaimed throughout the country for several years has had a great deal of influence on shop organizations, but *it has hardly been heeded at all in the financial and*

selling ends of business, where it is needed even worse than in the shops.

The cost keeping and accounting methods in general use in our industries today are so devised as to put all blame for failure on the producing portion of the business, and do not show the loss due to improper business policies, which it is safe to say are a more fertile source of failure than mistakes made by the production end of the business...

It is necessary that our cost keeping and accounting methods of the future shall show what losses are due to an unwise policy, or to poor management. In other words, our industrial scheme will not be rounded out until we have a means of measuring the ability with which those at the head of the business perform their functions, that is at least as good as that which we use to measure the efficiency of the operative [factory]...

The time will come, however, and indeed is not far distant, when cost keeping and accounting methods, which in the past have been so devised as to put all blame on the producer, will be so changed as to place blame for failure where it belongs, and give credit to whom credit is due." (pp. 38-40)

It sounds like Gantt's focus on blame and assigning proper responsibility comes from someone who has received more than his fair share of blame that did not belong to him, and he was sick of it. More importantly, Gantt was concerned about fundamental issues such as fairness and total business performance. He goes on to say:

> "Our difficulty in the past has been mainly with the commercial man, who has certain theories of efficiency gained form the cost accountant which are fatal to our efforts to make improvements of any kind." (p. 65)

The two theories that Gantt disliked the most were that "the expense of the supervising force must be small compared to that of those who are actually performing physical work;" that is, the indirect to direct labor ratio.

> "The result of this theory is that the foreman or superintendent who wishes to make a good showing in the eyes of the cost accountant has as large a pay roll as possible in order that the ratio of his salary and that of his clerks to the wages of the workman may be small." (p. 66)

The second theory was "the fallacy that it is necessary to have low wages in order to have low costs," as noted by Taylor previously.

Many of us can relate to Gantt's frustration. I remember when I was a manufacturing manager, and later as a purchasing manager, the computer system said the standard cost for a part was $700 – a number that was put into the system some ten or fifteen years earlier. But the actual current-day manufacturing cost or purchase price was $2000. So we would go to finance managers to request that the figure in the computer system be changed to reflect reality. The answer was always no, primarily because the variance was unfavorable. We had thousands of such data integrity issues.

It was not long before we figured out that finance was not interested in our reality – the reality of production – which included filling customer orders on-time and correcting errors in the cost accounting system. But they were fanatical about blaming me and holding me accountable to cost variances from which there was absolutely no hope of recovery.

Nor were they aware of the games played with the earned hours metric, which forces factory managers to dampen responsiveness to marketplace demand by converting buyers' market production work into sellers' market production work – in other words, make what earns you the most labor hours (sellers' market view) instead of making what customers ordered (buyers' market view).

Faced with completely unrealistic demands, people will get creative and find dozens of ways to cheat to survive the madness thrust upon them by senior management [10]. It is no surprise that costs were not reduced, and the manufacturing facility I worked in was eventually shut down. But what is a surprise is that the top finance and accounting managers seemed to be in the dark about how production and purchasing managers were gaming the metrics, and how these metrics completely disrupted the flow of products into buyers' markets.

Taiichi Ohno (1912-1990) also had some problems with accountants, and had this to say about anyone who blindly believed in the numbers [11]:

> "It is so easy to believe in the illusion that with a press, for example, it is much cheaper to stamp 10,000 pieces

using the same setup than 1,000 pieces. When this illusion is supported by numbers, people then believe the illusion is the truth.

It is so easy mathematically to 'prove' that it is inefficient, for example, not to stamp for at least two hours if the setup takes one hour: that producing more will reduce cost regardless of whether the setup takes ten minutes or an hour: or that the advantages of reducing the setup time to ten minutes are lost if the lot size is also reduced at the same time. These mathematical calculations are based on a completely different set of assumptions. It is useless to respond to them directly. The only thing we can say is: 'Yes, that's true as far as it goes' [meaning that it is valid only in the context of a mathematical calculation, and not valid in the context of the real world].

We [Toyota] always say to produce as much as can be sold and no more than that. When this is seen from a mathematical approach, people end up saying: 'What's wrong with you? Producing 20 instead of 10 reduces costs.' Ignoring the amount that can be sold and concentrating only on the cost-reducing potential [driven by volume] is a mistake frequently made by believers in mathematical calculation."

Ohno is admonishing those who cannot shake their belief in illusions. He chides managers whose business serves buyers' markets, but who make decisions based on the mistaken view that they serve sellers' markets. Saying "It is useless to respond to them directly" summarizes the frustration many of us have faced in trying to get managers and accountants to "go see" – and also to act upon what they have seen.

In his book *Workplace Management* [12], Ohno also lamented the fact that "intellectuals" had trouble understanding the profoundly different meanings of these two mathematically equivalent expressions:

  1) selling price = cost + profit
  2) selling price – cost = profit

Equation 1, favored by accounts, reflects a sellers' market view that the factory's output must bear all costs incurred by the business. As Taiichi Ohno put it, this "makes the customer responsible for every cost" [13]. It is a totally flawed way to manage if the company operates in competitive markets, which most do. Further, it promotes complacency with regards to internal cost reduction activities.

Equation 2 reflects a buyers' market in which buyers set the price, in recognition that the company does, if fact, operate in competitive markets. So in order to make a profit the company must reduce costs, which does promote hands-on shop and office floor cost reduction activities that all employees must participate in – even accountants.

Ohno goes on to say:

> "It seems to me that the biggest illusion for 'numbers-pushers' lies in departing from sophisticated calculations and thinking that simple arithmetic will show how many units must be sold for costs to drop...

> For us [engineers], costs are things to be lowered rather
> than things to be calculated… it is so difficult to win
> people over to our way of thinking."

In other words, it is more productive to engage people in cost
reduction activities than for them to be engaged in efforts to
calculate costs. He also suggests that we be weary of accountants who focus on unit costs:

> "When the accountant says that costs have been held
> down, it seems to me that, rather than swallowing their
> story whole, you have to look into whether real costs
> for the company have declined or not."

Ohno is, of course, advising us to understand total cost, rather
than simple unit cost savings in labor, manufacturing, or purchasing. To this day, enterprise software systems still focus on
unit costs and thus continue to mislead management and promote faulty decision-making.

> "Everyone has the impression that accounting is
> responsible for cost-cutting, but if you think about it,
> accounting is entirely incapable of reducing costs."

Ohno, and likely Taylor and Gantt, would probably be aston-
ished to learn how the business press today often characterizes
by-the-numbers finance executives as "operations wizards."

Returning to Ohno's comment, he is quite right in the classi-
cal sense of their job function; we have long thought of
finance and accounting people narrowly as focused on the
numbers and far removed from the actual value creating

activities. But we should no longer think of finance and accounting people that way. We should establish higher expectations of them as hands-on participants in cost reduction activities who possess detailed knowledge of Lean principles and practices. In other words, we have to get finance and accounting people – especially managers and executives – engaged in kaizen [14].

In his book *Toyota Production System* [15], Ohno was critical of the accounting terms such as "book value" and "depreciation" when it comes to making decisions about factory equipment:

> "…we often hear: 'This machine has been depreciated and paid off, and, therefore, we can discard it at any time without loss,' or 'The book value of this machine is zero. Why spend money on an overhaul when we can replace it with a new advanced model?'
>
> This kind of thinking is a big mistake… A machine's value is not determined by its years of service or its age. It is determined by the earning power it still retains…replacement of a machine is never cheaper, even if maintaining the older one entails some expense."

Ohno's animosity towards finance appears to have peaked in September 1978 when he was bumped from Toyota's board and his internal rival, finance vice president Masaya Hanai (1912-1995), became Chairman. According to Isao Shinohara [16]:

> "This incensed Ohno. Hanai had come up through the accounting side of the firm…As far as Ohno was con-

cerned, Toyota's present eminence as a company that
even Ford and General Motors were willing to learn
from resulted not from Toyota's solid accounting practices, but from the efforts made by the production, marketing, and sales departments.

Toyota is sometimes referred to as the 'Toyota Bank'
because of its robust financial condition. But, as far as
Ohno was concerned, the financial strength came about
because cars were produced and sold, not because
accounting had come up with the money. The accounting departments had just wisely managed the funds."

Teamwork among senior executives has its own challenges.
Ohno retired from Toyota Motor Corporation shortly there-
after but continued to serve as Chairman of Toyoda Spinning
and Weaving.

Finally, Ohno said [17]:

"We discovered that industry has to accept orders from
each customer and make products that differ according
to individual requirements."

This simple statement has enormous implications for finance
and accounting executives; it changes everything with regards
to their basic way of thinking, policies, management accounting, and performance metrics, all of which are closely aligned
with a sellers' market perspective – which is an illusion. At a
minimum, Ohno must have been happy that Mr. Hanai understood that Toyota operated in buyers' markets. That's an
advantage most operations vice presidents don't have.

We are fortunate that there are now many resources to help finance and accounting managers understand the changes that need to be made in their basic way thinking and managerial accounting practices [18-20]. But we must go further and help them understand the difference between office-based calculations, which may be mathematically correct, and shop and office floor work. Getting financial managers involved in kaizen and teaching them to "go see" will help them understand how paper-based calculations many not represent the actual facts. Doing so will also help them learn the value of the Lean management system [21]. If we are unable to do this, the strained relationship between accountants and production managers will go on for another hundred years.

Notes

[1] S.P. Garner, *The Evolution of Cost Accounting to 1925*, The University of Alabama Press, University, Alabama, 1954

[2] M. Epstein and J. Epstein, "An Annotated Bibliography of Scientific Management and Standard Costing to 1920," *Abacus*, Vol. 10, No. 2, 1974, pp. 165-174.

[3] J. Huntzinger, *Lean Cost Management: Accounting for Lean by Establishing Flow*, J. Ross Publishing, Ft. Lauderdale, FL, 2007

[4] "The Toyota Way 2001," Toyota Motor Corporation, internal document, Toyota City, Japan, April 2001

[5] F.W. Taylor, "Shop Management," *Transactions of The American Society of Mechanical Engineers*, Vol. 25, 1903, pp. 1337-1480

[6] F.W. Taylor, *The Principles of Scientific Management*, Harper & Brothers Publishers, New York, NY, 1911. In a nutshell, Scientific Management can be described as a system of production management that, if done correctly, resulted in a much more efficient batch-and-queue (push) production system; 2-3 times more efficient than basic batch-and-queue production. Its application was later extended to non-production activities and to non-manufacturing industries. Its main foci were "betterment" of the work and "cooperation," and some of its principles, methods, and tools are the same or similar to that found in Lean management. Scientific Management was an early attempt to create a non-zero-sum management system. Technically, however, it retains zero-sum features because it is still a batch-and-queue (push) system. However, Scientific Management is much less zero-sum compared to simple batch-and-queue management thinking and practice. The rationale for improved human relations and the work analysis methods developed by the leaders of Scientific Management (or separately by others) were major advances in management thinking and practice. To understand how Scientific Management served as the precursor to Lean management, see W. Tsutsui, *Manufacturing Ideology: Scientific Management in Twentieth-Century Japan*, Princeton University press, Princeton New Jersey, 1998.

[7] See *Manufacturing Costs and Accounts*, A.H. Church, McGraw-Hill Book Company, Inc., New York, NY, 1917

[8] See http://en.wikipedia.org/wiki/Henry_Gantt

[9] H.L. Gantt, *Industrial Leadership: Addresses Delivered in the Page Lecture Series, 1915, Before the Senior Class of The Sheffield Scientific School, Yale University*, Association Press, New York, NY, 1915

[10] M.L. Emiliani, D.J. Stec, and L.P. Grasso, "Unintended Responses to

a Traditional Purchasing Performance Metric," *Supply Chain Management: An International Journal*, Vol. 10, No. 3, 2005, pp. 150-156

[11] Interview of Taiichi Ohno in *NPS New Production System: JIT Crossing Industry Boundaries*, by I. Shinohara, Productivity Press, Norwalk, CT, 1985, p. 146-147

[12] T. Ohno, *Workplace Management*, Productivity press, Cambridge, MA, 1988, p. 21-24, 35, 143

[13] T. Ohno, *Toyota Production System*, Productivity Press, Portland, OR, 1988, p. 8

[14] B. Emiliani, with D. Stec, L. Grasso, and J. Stodder, *Better Thinking, Better Results: Case Study and Analysis of an Enterprise-Wide Lean Transformation,* second edition, The CLBM, LLC, Wethersfield, Conn., 2007

[15] Reference [13], p. 64

[16] I. Shinohara, *NPS New Production System: JIT Crossing Industry Boundaries*, Productivity Press, Norwalk, CT, 1985, p. 26-27

[17] Reference [13], p. xiv

[18] J. Cunningham and O. Fiume, *Real Numbers: Management Accounting in a Lean Organization*, Managing Times Press, Durham, NC, 2003

[19] B. Maskell and B. Baggaley, *Practical Lean Accounting*, Productivity Press, New York, NY, 2004

[20] J. Huntzinger, *Lean Cost Management: Accounting for Lean by Establishing Flow*, J. Ross Publishing, Ft. Lauderdale, FL, 2007

[21] Gantt complained that top managers did not do all they could to increase output from existing plants using Scientific Management, and instead took the easy way by spending money on new plants and equipment: "The man who can get a large product out of a small plant, is certainly in a better position to compete than he who requires a larger plant for the same output. This fact has been so often stated and so clearly demonstrated that it is hard to understand why it is so continuously ignored. Yet financiers, who as a rule determine policies, do not seem to have grasped the idea, and are in general much more willing to spend large sums of money on plant and equipment, rather than smaller sums in putting what they have in condition to get out a larger product. The explanation of this appears to be that the cost accountant of the past has invariably inventoried the new plant at cost, while he has not been able to place any inventory value on a system of management." Reference [9], pp. 123-24.

12 Memo to Finance Executives

*Finance executives are a key part of the leadership team
that helps drive a Lean transformation forward. They will
have to do a lot of Lean thinking in order to help out —
but that's not enough. Financial managers also will have
to acquire the unique beliefs, behaviors, and competencies
related to Lean management in order to be effective
participants and credible leaders.*

Ever since people became aware of the Toyota Production
System in the late 1970s and Toyota's overall management
system in the mid 1980s and early 1990s, executives seeking
to emulate Toyota have struggled with two principal elements: leadership and culture change. An important part of
this problem is embedded in the way businesses account for
costs [1], measure performance, and how finance organizations are led. Finance executives have to learn much more
about Lean than simply gaining book knowledge of what
waste is and the fundamentals of Lean accounting.

My first exposure to the leadership and culture change problem was in the summer of 1994, when I was a business unit
manager at Pratt & Whitney, a manufacturer of gas turbine
engines. Pratt was undergoing a Lean transformation under
the tutelage of Shingijutsu consultants. It was apparent rather
quickly that some line and staff managers where much better
than others at understanding and applying Lean principles
and practices. Further, some managers not only possessed a
better understanding, but they also exhibited noticeably different leadership behaviors that were more consistent with

Lean principles and practices.

Unfortunately, these types of managers were in the minority.
The majority of line and staff managers continued to lead the
way they had always led, apparently unable to see the need to
change or were unwilling to do so. They also tried to manage
with the same old financial metrics designed for batch-and
processes, such as earned hours and purchase price variance.

Regrettably, the finance executives were not helpful. They
continued to run the business using financial and non-financial measures designed for batch-and-queue production,
which reinforced conventional management thinking in the
middle of a Lean transformation. Operating managers were
forced to comply with the finance's rules and systems even
though we knew it was inconsistent with Lean, and nobody in
the central finance organization was interested in adopting the
Lean accounting we had devised at a local level to support
our new operating system.

These experiences propelled me on a fourteen-year mission
as both a management practitioner, and later as a practical
academic, to determine why effective Lean leadership and
culture change is so elusive, and what can be done to help get
finance and other executives on board. I devoted myself to
developing real-world concepts, methods, and tools that can
help any senior manager become an effective Lean leader.

Since 1998, I have written or co-written several practical
papers that describe how leaders must think and what they
must do differently if they expect to practice Lean successfully. The first paper, titled "Lean Behaviors," [2] showed that

there were two types of leadership behaviors; value-added and non-value-added-but-necessary behaviors [3], and waste (as in wasteful behaviors). I defined "behavioral waste" as behaviors that do not add value and can be eliminated. Examples of wasteful leadership behaviors include: perpetuating stereotypes, bullying, confusion, office politics, saying one thing and doing another, and blaming people for problems. These behaviors add cost but do not add any value. No end-use customer wants to pay for the delays and re-work caused by wasteful leadership behaviors.

Unfortunately, the biggest beatings I got as a business unit manager was when I didn't hit my numbers for the month, quarter, or end-of-year. The behavioral waste that the finance organization exhibited, deliberately or not, or caused other people to exhibit was truly remarkable [4].

Finance executives, or any other leader who tells associates to eliminate waste in processes, must be totally consistent and not behave in wasteful ways. In addition, leaders who adopt Lean management yet continue to behave in wasteful ways violate the "Respect for People" principle. Thus, my work to extend Taiichi Ohno's definitions of work and waste to the realm of leadership and leadership behaviors is simplicity itself and leads to an utterly practical solution to the Lean leadership problem. But it is only effective if leaders understand what waste is, and to get that understanding, they must participate in kaizen. Most finance executives don't do this, and hence our Lean leadership problem persists.

Another paper titled "Continuous Personal Improvement" showed how the exact same Lean tools that Lean businesses use to improve processes also can be used to develop and improve Lean leadership effectiveness [5]. This created a new approach that is simple and completely consistent with all Lean principles and practices. However, most finance executives don't understand the Lean tools because they have not participated in kaizen.

I soon realized that the papers I had written were a good start, but they were not good enough. It seemed that effective Lean leadership went beyond leadership behaviors and extended deeply into one's beliefs about various aspects of business and human relations. The beliefs of Lean leaders, it turns out, are indeed very different than the beliefs of leaders who manage businesses in a conventional (batch-and-queue) fashion. Finance executives, just like most other people, are strongly rooted in the conventional (batch-and-queue) ways of doing business.

So in my next paper, "Linking Leader's Beliefs to their Behaviors and Competencies" [6], I graphically illustrated the logical progression from beliefs to behaviors to competencies, where the competencies that leaders possess could be either good or bad. I showed how beliefs (something accepted as true) lead to certain predictable behaviors (conduct based upon beliefs), and that these behaviors lead to competencies (an established skill or capability). I showed the progression for both conventional leadership and Lean leadership. The contrast is striking and clearly shows how conventional beliefs-behaviors-competencies completely undercut Lean management. Since most CEOs and CFOs are strongly rooted in conventional (batch-and-queue) ways of thinking and doing business, it's no wonder why there are so few

REAL Lean transformations.

Published in 2003, this paper was a breakthrough because for the first time it made explicit what had for decades been implicit among the very best Lean practitioners. What once was inaccessible is now available to all Lean practitioners. It made the abstract nature of Lean leadership tangible, specific, and most importantly, actionable. But there is a problem; to gain the new Lean beliefs, the leaders must participate in kaizen. Once again kaizen is the key, but most finance executives don't do this.

While this was a major step forward, I felt that more needed to be done to make this approach even more practical and useful. Value stream maps, which had recently become popular, would be the key. And to help matters, many finance executives had begun to understand value stream maps.

Value stream maps, originally called "material and information flow diagrams," were developed by the Operations Management Consulting Division of Toyota Motor Corporation, Toyota City, Japan, in the late 1980s. They are one-page diagrams depicting the processes used to make a product and represent the collective current best practice for satisfying customer requirements. Current state value stream maps help identify ways to improve material and information flow, improve productivity and competitiveness, and help people implement system rather than isolated process improvements. For over ten years, value stream maps were applied principally to manufacturing activities. More recently, however, value stream maps have been used to understand the flow of material and information in service and office activities such as order entry, new product development, and financial reporting.

Brian Maskell and Bruce Baggaley recently extended the use of value stream maps to the field of finance and accounting to determine the process costs of a value stream [7]. The information contained in value stream maps is used to calculate current and future state process costs and create value stream profit-and-loss statements. This is a significant change from traditional standard cost accounting because it more accurately reflects the costs associated with production and non-production activities. David Simons and Robert Mason recently have used value stream maps to determine the amount of carbon dioxide greenhouse gas generated by processing and transportation [8].

Our paper "Using Value Stream Maps to Improve Leadership" [9] illustrates a fourth distinct use for value stream maps. It presents for the first time how value stream maps can be used to determine leadership beliefs, behaviors, and competencies. Current and future state value stream maps for manufacturing and service business processes illustrate the progression from belief to behavior to competency. Once again, the contrast is striking. It dramatically shows the vast difference between current state beliefs-behaviors-competencies compared with future state leadership beliefs-behaviors-competencies.

The significance of this paper is that it presents a high impact, practical, simple, and much less expensive route for identifying leadership problems and improving leadership effectiveness using diagrams and language that Lean practitioners already understand.

Finance and accounting executives who comprehend these four papers will better understand how their accounting systems, practices, and metrics support current state batch-and-queue material or information processing, in addition to batch-and-queue oriented leadership routines used in the finance organization and how other people in the company perceive them. As you know, financial systems and conventional performance metrics are rooted in batch-and-queue thinking and have been with us for over one hundred years [1]. They do not support businesses that seek to compete on the basis of time, nor do most financial processes or leadership practices of finance executives.

That is why finance executives cannot simply offer their support for Lean. Gaining book knowledge of what waste is and the fundamentals of Lean accounting and not enough either. They have to learn by doing and change the ways they think, behave, and make decisions.

Current state beliefs perpetuate dysfunctional leadership behaviors and reinforce daily use of competencies that yield outcomes the opposite of those desired by senior managers. They disable communication and learning within the organization and between companies. The flow of information is impeded, which leads to repetitive errors, causes systemic problems to go undetected, and inhibits overall system improvement. It also contributes to a distorted view of reality, wasteful organizational politics, and blaming people when things go wrong. None of this benefits customers, the source of sales and cash flow.

Future state beliefs result in entirely different leadership behaviors and competencies, which are then modeled by mid-level managers and associates and thus result in highly desirable organizational capabilities. In other words, they lead to the creation of a culture that is energetic and imaginative, questions processes, supports rapid improvement, collaborates to understand problems and identifies countermeasures, and recognizes that organizational politics and blaming people are waste. What also emerges is a much more accurate view of reality, in part due to the elimination of financial and non-financial performance metrics rooted in batch-and-queue thinking.

Importantly, the future state consumes much less resources of all types; physical, mental, money, plant, property, equipment, raw material, services, etc. Finance executives ought to be very interested in achieving that. The future state is also much more responsive to changes in customers' desires. To access all of these good things, finance executives cannot just delegate the understanding of current and future-state beliefs-behaviors-competencies to lower-level managers and associates. They have to learn it themselves. This will surely be a challenge for finance executives, many of whom, it seems, feel they have little to learn.

Hopefully, you will get much more involved in the Lean transformation and understand deeper aspects and nuances of the Lean management system [10-15]. Finance executives should want to be a catalyst for the positive changes that are necessary to achieve REAL Lean. But first they have to understand and question their current state beliefs about finance and accounting, related systems and practices, financial and non-financial performance metrics, decision-making, etc.

There is not doubt this will be very uncomfortable because some of what you now know will no longer be relevant. However, the discomfort is necessary in order to shift an enterprise to a better future state, one that has no need for bad metrics and zero-sum financial engineering [16].

Notes

[1] Standard cost accounting was developed in support of the batch-and-queue production method that was used to serve sellers' markets circa 1900. It was created to specifically address costs in large industrial enterprises (vs. craft enterprises) related to idleness of man and machine (production capacity issues and overhead costs), fluctuating prices of purchased materials, and when large numbers of discrete purchase orders are made over time. The creation of standard costs is an averaging function designed to make the accountant's job easier. See *Manufacturing Costs and Accounts*, A.H. Church, McGraw-Hill Book Company, Inc., New York, NY, 1917; *The Evolution of Cost Accounting to 1925*, S.P. Garner, The University of Alabama Press, University, Alabama, 1954; "An Annotated Bibliography of Scientific Management and Standard Costing to 1920," M. Epstein and J. Epstein, *Abacus*, Vol. 10, No. 2, 1974, pp. 165-174. Standard cost accounting is inappropriate for Lean production, which is designed to serve buyers' markets. See *Real Numbers: Management Accounting in a Lean Organization*, J. Cunningham and O. Fiume, Managing Times Press, Durham, NC, 2003 and *Practical Lean Accounting*, B. Maskell and B. Baggaley, Productivity Press, New York, NY, 2004

[2] M.L. Emiliani, "Lean Behaviors," *Management Decision*, Vol. 36, No. 9, pp. 615-631, 1998. Emiliani coined the term "Lean Behaviors" in August 1996.

[3] Non-value added but necessary behaviors can also be thought of as unavoidable behaviors because people are not perfect.

[4] Every CEO, president, and finance executive needs to understand – in detail – the games people play with metrics. Finance executives should not blame people for the games. Instead, they should eliminate or de-emphasize metrics that cause waste, unevenness, and unreasonableness. Standard costs, earned hours, purchase price variance, machine utilization, and earned value systems are among the worst metrics. See for example, M.L. Emiliani, D.J. Stec, and L.P. Grasso, "Unintended Responses to a Traditional Purchasing Performance Metric," *Supply Chain Management: An International Journal*, Vol. 10, No. 3, 2005, pp. 150-156

[5] M.L. Emiliani, "Continuous Personal Improvement," *Journal of Workplace Learning*, Vol. 10, No. 1, pp. 29-38, 1998

[6] M.L. Emiliani, "Linking Leaders' Beliefs to Their Behaviors and Competencies," *Management Decision*, Vol. 41, No. 9, pp. 893-910, 2003

[7] *Practical Lean Accounting*, B. Maskell and B. Baggaley, Productivity Press, New York, NY, 2004

[8] D. Simons and R. Mason, "Lean and Green: "Doing More with Less," *ECR Journal*, Vol. 3, No. 1, Spring 2003, pp. 84-91

[9] M.L. Emiliani and D.J. Stec, "Using Value Stream Maps to Improve Leadership," *Leadership and Organizational Development Journal*, Vol. 25, No. 8, pp. 622-645, 2004

[10] M.L. Emiliani, "Origins of Lean Management in America: The Role of Connecticut Businesses", *Journal of Management History*, Vol. 12, No. 2, pp. 167-184, 2006, http://www.theclbm.com/articles/lean_in_conn.pdf

[11] B. Emiliani, with D. Stec, L. Grasso, and J. Stodder, *Better Thinking, Better Results: Case Study and Analysis of an Enterprise-Wide Lean Transformation*, second edition, The CLBM, LLC, Wethersfield, Conn., 2007

[12] B. Emiliani, *REAL LEAN: Understanding the Lean Management System*, Volume One, The CLBM, LLC, Wethersfield, Conn., 2007,

[13] T. Ohno, *Toyota Production System*, Productivity Press, Portland, OR, 1988

[14] S. Hino, *Inside the Mind of Toyota*, Productivity Press, New York, NY, 2006

[15] J. Liker, *The Toyota Way*, McGraw-Hill, New York, NY, 2004

[16] Examples of include layoffs, plant and office closings, squeezing suppliers, channel stuffing, price fixing, to name just a few.

13 Lean Enterprise Estate Planning

Let's say you are the president or CEO and you have done a good job creating the beginnings of a Lean enterprise over the past ten or twenty years. What are you going to do to ensure that the customer-first organization you helped create will survive your retirement or other major change? It is time to do some Lean enterprise estate planning.

It is inevitable. Someday you will retire, new senior managers will be hired from the outside, or perhaps the business will one day be sold or merged with another company. How will you perpetuate the wealth creating business you once led? How will you avoid the merger and acquisition culture clash that so often leads to a loss of control and disruptive changes in management practice? How will you ensure high fidelity continuity in the practice of the Lean management system that you helped to establish?

Many senior managers think that Lean management, if practiced for just five to ten years, will "stick" and become self-sustaining. This will never happen. The unrelenting force of batch-and-queue gravity will always return a Lean business to the old way of thinking and doing. Toyota is no different; they have to fight every day against the force of batch-and-queue gravity and complacency [1].

In addition, The Wiremold Company's Lean transformation and subsequent backslide under new ownership [2], in addition to the many examples presented in Chapter 4, prove that it is nearly impossible to maintain continuity in the new non-zero-sum management system when senior managers change or when the business is sold or merged with another company.

Lean management lives in people. It is people who make Lean come alive and who keep Lean alive. When the people who know Lean management go away, Lean usually goes away with them.

The question is: what can you do to help ensure that your efforts are not reversed by the next generation of senior managers, or the one after that? For your company to survive this threat, you must plan ahead. If you are truly committed to Lean, you will make detailed preparations to ensure long-term continuity in Lean thinking and practice.

Here are some things you must ask yourself:

- Have we determined our corporate purpose [3]? Have we made it explicit [4]? Does everyone understand it? Are we bringing our corporate purpose to life every day? If not, why not?
- Have we established non-zero-sum business principles [5]? Have we made them explicit [6]? Does everyone understand the principles? Are we bringing our business principles to life every day? If not, why not?
- Are we committed to training explicit aspects of Lean knowledge – both on-the-job and in the classroom? How do we know?
- Are we committed to the human transfer of tacit Lean knowledge from one generation to the next? How do we know?

How will you hold senior managers accountable to these things ten, fifty, or one hundred years from now? Should corporate by-laws be amended to reflect REAL Lean as the management system?

What is the penalty if a future CEO decides to negate the corporation's purpose? What is the penalty for adopting zero-sum business principles? What is the penalty for cutting the Lean training budget to zero? What is the penalty for minimizing tacit Lean knowledge and instead reverting to the view that Lean is nothing more than a bunch of tools to improve efficiency? Do you penalize senior managers in the pocketbook? Do you demote them? Do you fire them? Do you re-train them? What will you do?

How do you establish a one hundred-plus year commitment to promoting people from within, based on merit, those people who excel at understanding and applying Lean principles and practices, and not based on favoritism or politics?

When you hire people from the outside, should you make learning and practicing Lean management part of the employment contract for senior managers? How will you know they are practicing "Continuous Improvement" and "Respect for People" every day?

If the company must change hands, how do you ensure it sold to a buyer who has demonstrated commitment to Lean management, REAL Lean, and not to a buyer who promises to become committed to Lean in the future.

What if the company that wants to buy your business is much

bigger and they are not Lean? Should you create a plan
whereby the Lean sensei, your senior managers, train the students, the acquiring company's senior managers? Will senior
managers of the acquiring company ever see themselves as
students? Will their egos let them do that? If, from a practical
perspective, the answer is "no," then what will you do?

Should you make your Lean management system part of the
merger contract? Would it include rights to reject batch-and-
queue thinking and practice handed down to you from the
parent company? How do you enforce that? Alternatively,
should you consider buying the company that wants to buy
you and make them become Lean?

Should you instead sell the business to its managers in a management buy-out, or to its employees to make it an employ-
ee-owned company? Should you take the company private if
it is publicly owned, or have an initial public offering of stock
if it is privately owned? If you do the latter, you should carefully follow Toyota's lead on how they manage their
investors' expectations.

Like your own personal estate planning in which you are
committed to ensuring the future prosperity of your survivors,
the leaders of a Lean business also must make similar preparations. Failure to do so will mean that managers' and associates' dedicated efforts, and the company's end-use customers,
will begin to disappear.

Notes

[1] See "No Satisfaction at Toyota," C. Fishman, *Fast Company*, Issue 111, December 2006, http://www.fastcompany.com/magazine/111/open_no-satisfaction.html; "Top Spot In Sight, Toyota Not Slacking," I. Rowley, *BusinessWeek*, 13 December 2006, http://www.businessweek.com/globalbiz/content/dec2006/gb20061213_806308.htm; and "The Man Driving Toyota," P. O'Connell, *BusinessWeek*, 22 July 2005, http://www.businessweek.com/bwdaily/dnflash/jul2005/nf20050721_7169_db053.htm

[2] B. Emiliani, with D. Stec, L. Grasso, and J. Stodder, *Better Thinking, Better Results: Case Study and Analysis of an Enterprise-Wide Lean Transformation*, second edition, The CLBM, LLC, Wethersfield, Conn., 2007

[3] S. Basu, *Corporate Purpose: Why it Matters More than Strategy*, Garland Publishing, New York, NY, 1999

[4] http://www.toyota.co.jp/en/vision/message/index.html, as well as http://www.toyota.co.jp/en/vision/philosophy/index.html and

http://www.toyota.co.jp/en/vision/sustainability/index.html

[5] "The Toyota Way 2001," Toyota Motor Corporation, internal document, Toyota City, Japan, April 2001

[6] "Caux Round Table: *Principles for Business*," http://www.cauxroundtable.org/documents/Principles%20for%20Business.PDF

Afterword

I hope you have found the second volume of REAL LEAN to be informative, practical, and helpful in identifying the critical issues and opportunities in Lean management. I also hope that this book motivates you to learn more about the Lean management system and inspires you to practice every day, even if only in a few small ways. If not, then perhaps it is because you think your situation is unique in some way.

We tend to think our circumstances are significantly different from others because we work in different departments, in different companies, or in different industries; and what worked for one manager or company will not work for any other. At a conference in 1911, Mr. F.G. Patterson, an auditor for Pacific and Atlantic Mills in Boston, Massachusetts, cites a simple fact of business that each new generation of managers have great difficulty accepting [1]:

> "Everybody thinks that the need of his particular industry is different from that of any other, and that his problems will have to be met separately. As a rule, the problems in the majority of these various kinds of businesses are all the same, though called by different names, – talked about in different languages. The solutions are largely the same."

At the same conference noted engineer and consultant Mr. Sanford Thompson said [2]:

> "It is almost laughable, the way any man... will make

> the same remark as another man, that 'it is applicable in
> your shop, but cannot be done in my shop, because my
> conditions are entirely different, and too intricate'."

Our circumstances seem unique to us because we are experiencing them for the first time, and we tend to ignore the experiences and advice of our predecessors. However, if you take the long view that history provides, we find that our circumstances are the same or very similar to what others experienced years ago. And so if we are serious about improvement, it is wise to observe what management practitioners did before our time, through their writings, and understand why they did what they did and how they did it. This will help us better understand the context of their challenges; what led to their successes; the failures they experienced; and how they tried to correct them.

William Redfield, a United States Congressman from New York and president of American Blower Company, said at the same conference in 1911 [3]:

> "The greatest curse the American manufacturer has is
> knowing his own business. It is a disease of the brain...
> Years ago a very successful partner, and older man than
> I and wiser, laid down this rule to me as his junior...
> 'Every manufacturer should always and continuously
> be his own severest critic. He should always be finding
> fault with himself. He should never be satisfied, and he
> should never let his business get into such a condition
> that any customer can find fault with him. That shows
> he doesn't know his job. At the end of 20 years of practice I begin to realize that I know very little about this

business… Redfield… please take an hour every day and go out into the shop and find all the fault you can.' To the man who says to me, 'I know my own business,' I say in my own mind, 'God help you'."

The same words apply to service businesses, government, non-profits, etc. Once again, there is much to learn from our predecessors. Their insights remain highly relevant to today's challenge of advancing REAL Lean management.

Several chapters highlight the difference between zero-sum and non-zero sum thinking found in conventionally managed businesses compared to Lean businesses. I hope this contrast comes through clearly to all readers because it is a principal mode by which Lean transformations fail. It transcends the tools and methods which some view as essential to sustaining Lean management and Lean leadership.

Executives who carry forward traditional zero-sum thinking into the world of Lean management, and who do not plan for the future possibility that zero-sum thinking will creep into the business, are certain to fail. It does not matter which functional area an executive is responsible for; human resources, sales, engineering, marketing, finance, operations, legal, etc. Zero-sum thinking poisons Lean management, and will surely become a primary cause of failure.

Unfortunately, failure looms large for most practitioners of Lean management. That should not discourage you. Instead, it should motivate you to understand the root causes of others' failures, and identify and implement countermeasures so that you can avoid failure.

It will help greatly if you accept, completely and without
any doubt, that the best Lean leaders are realists. They say
to themselves:

> "Why would we do anything that works against our
> interests and the interests of our stakeholders? We
> know from experience that if we treat them poorly, they
> will seek to get even with us sometime in the future. So
> let's not do things to ourselves and to our stakeholders
> that create waste, unevenness, and unreasonableness."

Despite their strong protests, the leaders of conventionally
managed businesses are actually idealists. They say things like:

> "We need to reduce our costs. So let's force suppliers to
> lower their prices, close plants and offices, cut employ-
> ee pay and benefits, and lay people off. This will help
> ensure the company's survival."

Seeking long-term survival through zero-sum thinking and
actions is not practical.

Notes

[1] "Round Table Discussions: The Application of Scientific Management in Certain Industries," in *Scientific Management: First Conference at the Amos Tuck School Dartmouth College*, The Plimpton Press, Norwood, Mass, 1912, p. 180

[2] "Phases of Scientific Management: A Symposium," *Scientific Management: First Conference at the Amos Tuck School Dartmouth College*, The Plimpton Press, Norwood, Mass, 1912, p. 347

[3] Ibid, pp. 352-353

About the Author

M.L. "Bob" Emiliani is a professor at Connecticut State University in New Britain, Conn., where he teaches various courses on Lean management.

He worked in the consumer products and aerospace industries for nearly two decades and held management positions in engineering, manufacturing, and supply chain management, and had responsibility for implementing Lean in manufacturing operations and supply chains.

Emiliani has authored or co-authored a dozen papers related to Lean leadership including: "Lean Behaviors" (1998), "Linking Leaders' Beliefs to their Behaviors and Competencies" (2003), "Using Value Stream Maps to Improve Leadership" (2004), "Origins of Lean Management in America: The Role of Connecticut Businesses" (2006), and "Standardized Work for Executive Leadership (2008). Five of his papers have won awards for excellence.

He is the principal author of the book *Better Thinking, Better Results: Case Study and Analysis of an Enterprise-Wide Lean Transformation*, (second edition, 2007), a detailed case study and analysis of The Wiremold Company's Lean transformation from 1991 to 2001. It won a Shingo Research Prize in 2003 as the first book to describe an enterprise-wide Lean transformation in a real company where both principles of Lean management – "Continuous Improvement" and "Respect for People" – were applied.

He is also the author of *REAL LEAN: Understanding the Lean Managment System* (Volume One), published in 2007, *REAL LEAN: The Keys to Sustaining Lean Management* (Volume Three), published in 2008, and *Practical Lean Leadership: A Strategic Leadership Guide For Executives*, published in 2008.

Emiliani holds engineering degrees from the University of Miami, the University of Rhode Island, and Brown University.

He is the owner of The Center for Lean Business Management, LLC. (www.theclbm.com).